STUDY GUIDE

Volume I, Chapters 1-12

for use with

FUNDAMENTAL ACCOUNTING PRINCIPLES

Fourteenth Edition

Kermit D. Larson
University of Texas-Austin

Contributing Author

Barbara Chiappetta
Nassau Community College

IRWIN

Chicago • Bogotá • Boston • Buenos Aires • Caracas
London • Madrid • Mexico City • Sydney • Toronto

©Richard D. Irwin, a Times Mirror Higher Education Group, Inc. company, 1955, 1959, 1963, 1966, 1969, 1972, 1975, 1978, 1981, 1984, 1987, 1990, 1993, and 1996

Printed in the United States of America.

ISBN 0–256–16933–0

2 3 4 5 6 7 8 9 0 WCB 2 1 0 9 8 7 6

To the Student

This booklet is designed to help you review the material covered in *Fundamental Accounting Principles*. You should understand that the booklet is not intended to substitute for your review of *Fundamental Accounting Principles*. Instead, the objectives of this booklet are as follows:

1. To remind you of important information that is explained in the text. For example, the topical outline of each chapter reminds you of important topics in the chapter. In reading the outline, you should ask yourself whether or not you understand sufficiently the listed topics. If not, you should return to the appropriate chapter in *Fundamental Accounting Principles* and read carefully the portions that explain the topics about which you are unclear.

2. To provide you with a quick means of testing your knowledge of the chapter. If you are unable to correctly answer the problems that follow the chapter outline, you should again return to the appropriate chapter in *Fundamental Accounting Principles* and review the sections about which you are unclear.

Your best approach to the use of this booklet is as follows:

First, read the learning objectives and the related summary paragraphs. Then, ask whether your understanding of the chapter seems adequate for you to accomplish the objectives.

Second, review the topical outline, taking time to think through (describing to yourself) the explanations that would be required to expand the outline. Return to *Fundamental Accounting Principles* to cover areas of weakness.

Third, answer the requirements of the problems that follow the topical outline. Then, check your answers against the solutions that are provided after the problems.

Fourth, return to *Fundamental Accounting Principles* for further study of the portions of the chapter about which you made errors.

Table of Contents

Prologue

Your Introduction to
Business, Accounting, and Ethics

Learning Objective 1:

Describe the main purpose of accounting and its role in organizations.

Summary

The main purpose of accounting is to provide useful information to people who make rational investment, credit, and similar decisions. These decision makers include present and potential investors, lenders, and other users. The other users include managers of organizations, suppliers who sell to them, and customers who buy from them. Internally, accounting provides information that managers use in the following areas of activity: finance, human resources, research and development, production, marketing, and executive management.

Learning Objective 2:

Describe the external role of accounting for organizations.

Summary

In addition to using accounting information to meet internal needs, organizations also report accounting information to various external parties. These external decision makers include people who invest in the organizations and people who loan money to them. Lenders need information to assess whether the company has enough financial strength and profitability to pay its debts.

Learning Objective 3:

List the main fields of accounting and the activities carried on in each field.

Summary

Accountants work in private, public, and government accounting. All three have members who work in financial, managerial, and tax accounting. Financial accountants prepare or audit financial statements that are distributed to people who are not involved in day-to-day management. Managerial accountants provide information to people who are involved in day-to-day management. Managerial accounting activities include general accounting, cost accounting, budgeting, internal auditing, and management advisory services. Tax accounting includes preparing tax returns and tax planning.

Learning Objective 4:

State several reasons for the importance of ethics in accounting.

Summary

Ethics are principles that determine the rightness or wrongness of particular acts or activities. Ethics are also principles of conduct that govern an individual or a profession. The foundation for trust in business activities is the expectation that people are trustworthy. Ethics are especially important for accounting because users of the information have to trust that it has not been manipulated. Without ethics, accounting information could not be trusted, and economic activity would be much more difficult to accomplish.

Learning Objective 5:

Define or explain the words and phrases listed in the Prologue glossary.

Summary

See Problem I.

Topical Outline

I. The main purpose of accounting and its internal and external roles

   A. The main purpose of accounting is to provide useful financial information to decision makers so they can make better decisions. Because of this, accounting is often described as a "service activity."

   B. The internal role of accounting is to serve all of the other departments in the organization by providing them with useful information that helps them complete their tasks.

      1. Finance departments need cash flow information to project future cash flows.

      2. Human resources departments need information about employees and payroll costs.

      3. Research and development departments need cost reports so they can make decisions about continuing projects.

      4. Production departments need information about operating costs, and must follow internal control procedures provided by the accounting department.

      5. Marketing departments need information about sales and marketing costs.

      6. Executive managers depend on financial statements, budgets, and performance reports to make major decisions for the organization, develop long-term strategies, motivate employees, and deal with the public or the owners.

   C. The external role of accounting is to provide useful information to decision makers outside of the organization, such as potential investors and lenders, owners who are not managers, suppliers and customers, and government agencies that regulate business activities or collect taxes.

II. Recording and analyzing accounting information

   A. The difference between accounting and bookkeeping

      1. Bookkeeping is the clerical part of accounting that records transactions and other events.

      2. Accounting includes identifying how transactions and events should be described in financial statements, and designing and implementing systems to control the operations of an organization, all of which require more professional expertise and judgment than bookkeeping.

   B. Accounting and computers

      1. Computers are widely used in accounting because they can quickly and efficiently store, process, and summarize large quantities of financial data.

      2. However, there is still a need for people who can design accounting systems, supervise their operation, analyze complex transactions, and interpret reports.

III. The types and fields of accounting

   A. The three types of accountants

      1. Private accountants work for a single employer, usually a business.

      2. Public accountants offer their services to the public, and therefore work for many different clients. They may be self-employed or work for a public accounting firm.

      3. Government accountants are employed by local, state, and federal government agencies.

B. The three fields of accounting

   1. Financial accounting

      a. Private financial accountants prepare financial statements.

      b. Public financial accountants audit financial statements.

      c. Government financial accountants prepare financial statements, review financial reports, write regulations, assist businesses, and investigate violations.

   2. Managerial accounting

      a. Private managerial accountants perform activities such as general accounting (which includes financial accounting), cost accounting, budgeting, and internal auditing.

      b. Public managerial accountants provide management advisory services.

      c. Government managerial accountants, like private managerial accountants, perform general accounting, cost accounting, budgeting, and internal auditing functions.

   3. Tax accounting

      a. Private tax accountants prepare tax returns and assist in tax planning.

      b. Public tax accountants also prepare tax returns and assist in tax planning.

      c. Government tax accountants review tax returns, assist taxpayers, write regulations, and investigate violations.

IV. Ethics in accounting

A. Decision makers must be able to trust that the information in financial statements and other accounting reports has not been manipulated, and that the accountant is protecting their interests. When trust is lacking, our commercial and personal lives are much more complicated, inefficient, and unpleasant.

B. Ethics codes for accountants have been adopted and enforced by professional organizations, including the American Institute of Public Accountants (AICPA) and the Institute of Management Accountants (IMA).

Problem I

Many of the important ideas and concepts discussed in the prologue are reflected in the following list of key terms. Test your understanding of these terms by matching the appropriate definitions with the terms. Record the number identifying the most appropriate definition in the blank space next to each term.

_____	Accounting	_____	General accounting
_____	AICPA	_____	Generally accepted accounting principles
_____	Audit		
_____	Bookkeeping	_____	Government accountants
_____	Budgeting	_____	Internal auditing
_____	CIA	_____	IRS
_____	CMA	_____	Management advisory services
_____	Controller	_____	NASBA
_____	Cost accounting	_____	Private accountant
_____	CPA	_____	Public accountants
_____	Ethics	_____	SEC
_____	GAAP	_____	Tax accounting

1. American Institute of Certified Public Accountants; the largest and most influential national professional organization of Certified Public Accountants in the United States.

2. A service activity that provides useful information to people who make rational investment, credit, and similar decisions to help them make better decisions.

3. The field of accounting that includes preparing tax returns and planning future transactions to minimize the amount of tax; involves private, public, and government accountants.

4. An activity that adds credibility to reports produced and used within an organization; internal auditors not only examine record-keeping processes but also assess whether managers are following established operating procedures.

5. The process of developing formal plans for future activities, which then serve as a basis for evaluating actual performance.

6. A managerial accounting activity designed to help managers identify, measure, and control operating costs.

7. The chief accounting officer of an organization.

8. Rules adopted by the accounting profession as guides for measuring and reporting the financial condition and activities of a business.

9. A thorough check of an organization's accounting systems and records that adds credibility to financial statements; the specific goal is to determine whether the statements reflect the company's financial position and operating results in agreement with generally accepted accounting principles.

10. The public accounting activity in which suggestions are offered for improving a company's procedures; the suggestions may concern new accounting and internal control systems, new computer systems, budgeting, and employee benefit plans.

11. Securities and Exchange Commission; the federal agency created by Congress in 1934 to regulate securities markets, including the flow of information from companies to the public.

12. The part of accounting that records transactions and other events, either manually or with computers.

13. Certified Public Accountant; an accountant who has passed an examination and has met education and experience requirements; licensed by a state board to practice public accounting.

14. The task of recording transactions, processing the recorded data, and preparing reports for managers; also includes preparing the financial statements that executive management presents to external users.

15. The abbreviation for generally accepted accounting principles.

16. Certified Internal Auditor; a certification that an individual is professionally competent in internal auditing; granted by the Institute of Internal Auditors.

17. Internal Revenue Service; the federal agency that has the duty of collecting federal taxes and otherwise enforcing tax laws.

18. National Association of State Boards of Accountancy.

19. Certificate in Management Accounting; a certification that an individual is professionally competent in managerial accounting; awarded by the Institute of Management Accountants.

20. Accountants employed by local, state, and federal government agencies.

21. Accountants who provide their services to many different clients.

22. An accountant who works for a single employer, which is often a business.

23. Principles that determine the rightness or wrongness of particular acts or activities; also accepted standards of good behavior in a profession or trade.

Solutions for Prologue

Problem I

1 Financial Statements and Accounting Principles

Learning Objective 1:

Describe the information presented in financial statements, be able to prepare simple financial statements, and analyze a company's performance with the return on equity ratio.

Summary

The income statement shows a company's revenues, expenses, and net income or loss. The balance sheet lists a company's assets, liabilities, and owner's equity. The statement of changes in owner's equity shows the effects on owner's equity from investments by the owner, withdrawals, and net income or net loss. The statement of cash flows shows the changes that resulted from operating, investing, and financing activities. The financial statements are prepared with information about the effects of each transaction on the accounting equation. The company's performance can be analyzed by comparing the company's return on equity with rates on other investments available to the owner.

Learning Objective 2:

Explain the accounting principles introduced in the chapter and describe the process by which generally accepted accounting principles are established.

Summary

Accounting principles help accountants produce relevant and reliable information. Among others, broad accounting principles include the business entity principle, the objectivity principle, the cost principle, the going-concern principle, and the revenue recognition principle. Specific accounting principles for financial accounting are established in the United States primarily by the Financial Accounting Standards Board (FASB), with oversight by the Securities and Exchange Commission (SEC). Auditing standards are established by the Auditing Standards Board (ASB), a committee of the American Institute of CPAs (AICPA). The International Accounting Standards Committee (IASC) identifies preferred practices and encourages their adoption throughout the world.

Learning Objective 3:

Describe single proprietorships, partnerships, and corporations, including any differences in the owners' responsibilities for the debts of the organizations.

Summary

A single (or sole) proprietorship is an unincorporated business owned by one individual. A partnership differs from a single proprietorship in that it has more than one owner. Proprietors and partners are personally responsible for the debts of their businesses. A corporation is a separate legal entity. As such, its owners are not personally responsible for its debts.

Learning Objective 4:

Analyze business transactions to determine their effects on the accounting equation.

Summary

The accounting equation states that Assets = Liabilities + Owner's Equity. Business transactions always have at least two effects on the elements in the accounting equation. The accounting equation is always in balance when business transactions are properly recorded.

Learning Objective 5:

Define or explain the words and phrases listed in the chapter glossary.

Summary

See Problem III.

Topical Outline

I. Financial statements

    A. The income statement indicates whether a business earned a profit by showing:

        1. Revenues—inflows of assets received in exchange for goods or services provided to customers as part of the major or central operations of the business.

        2. Expenses—outflows or the using up of assets as a result of the major or central operations of a business.

        3. Net income (excess of revenues over expenses) or net loss (excess of expenses over revenues) for a period.

    B. The balance sheet provides information about a company's financial status as of a specific date by showing:

        1. Assets—properties or economic resources owned by the business; probable future economic benefits obtained or controlled by a particular entity as a result of past transactions or events.

        2. Liabilities—debts owed by a business or organization; probable future sacrifices of economic benefits arising from present obligations of a particular entity to transfer assets or provide services to other entities in the future as a result of past transactions or events.

        3. Equity—the difference between a company's assets and its liabilities; the residual interest in the assets of an entity that remains after deducting its liabilities; also called net assets.

    C. The statement of changes in owner's equity shows the beginning and ending balances of owner's equity for a period, and the items that caused the net change, including:

        1. Increases due to investments by the owner or net income.

        2. Decreases due to withdrawals by the owner or a net loss.

    D. The statement of cash flows describes where a company's cash came from and where it went during a period. The cash flows are classified as being caused by operating, investing, and financing activities.

II. Generally accepted accounting principles (GAAP) and generally accepted auditing standards (GAAS)

    A. GAAP include both broad and specific principles. The broad principles discussed in this book are:

        1. Business entity principle—every business is to be accounted for separately and distinctly from its owner or owners.

        2. Objectivity principle—financial statement information is to be supported by evidence other than someone's opinion or imagination.

        3. Cost principle—financial statements are to present information based on costs incurred in business transactions; assets and services are to be recorded initially at the cash or cash-equivalent amount given in exchange.

        4. Going-concern principle—financial statements are to reflect the assumption that the business will continue operating instead of being closed or sold, unless evidence shows that it will not continue.

        5. Revenue recognition principle—revenue should be recognized at the time it is earned; the inflow of assets associated with revenue may be in a form other than cash; and the amount of revenue should be measured as the cash plus the cash equivalent value of any noncash assets received from customers in exchange for goods or services.

        6. The time period, matching, materiality, full-disclosure, consistency, and conservatism principles are discussed in later chapters.

B. Organizations involved in developing GAAP and GAAS

    1. The Financial Accounting Standards Board (FASB) is the primary authoritative source for establishing new accounting principles, which are published in its Statements of Financial Accounting Standards (SFAS).

    2. Other professional organizations support the FASB's process with input and financial support, including the American Accounting Association (AAA), Financial Executives Institute (FEI), Institute of Management Accountants (IMA), Association for Investment Management and Research (AIMR), and the Securities Industry Association (SIA).

    3. Prior to FASB, the accounting profession depended on the Accounting Principles Board (APB), from 1959 to 1973, and the Committee on Accounting Procedure (CAP), from 1936 to 1959, to identify GAAP.

    4. The Auditing Standards Board (ASB) is a special committee of the AICPA and is the authority for identifying GAAS. The SEC is an important source of the ASB's authority.

C. In an effort to increase harmony among the accounting practices of different countries, accounting organizations from around the world have created the International Accounting Standards Committee (IASC) to identify preferred accounting practices and encourage their worldwide acceptance.

III. Legal forms of business organizations

A. Single proprietorship—an unincorporated business owned by one individual; the owner is personally responsible for the debts of the business.

B. Partnership—an unincorporated business that is owned by two or more people; the partners are personally responsible for the debts of the business.

C. Corporation—a business established as a separate legal entity under state or federal laws; the owners (stockholders) are not responsible for the debts of the business.

D. Differences in the financial statements

    1. On the balance sheet, proprietorships and partnerships list the names of the owners and their capital balances in the owner's equity section. The capital balances are the accumulation of owner investments and withdrawals as well as net incomes and losses. A corporation's equity section is called stockholders' equity, and is made up of contributed capital (owner investments from sales of stock) and retained earnings (the accumulation of net incomes and losses, reduced by dividends to the stockholders).

    2. Because a corporation is a separate legal entity, salaries paid to managers are reported as expenses on the income statement. However, if the owners of proprietorships or partnerships perform managerial services in the operations of the business, there is no expense reported on the income statement for their services. (If owners withdraw cash from the business, their capital accounts are reduced.)

IV. The accounting equation and recording transactions

A. The accounting equation (or balance sheet equation) is a way of describing the relationship between a company's assets, liabilities, and equity. It is expressed as: Assets = Liabilities + Owner's Equity.

B. When business transactions are properly recorded, they always have at least two effects on the accounting equation, and the equation always remains in balance.

V. Return on equity ratio

    A. One way to judge a business's relative success is to compare its return on equity ratio to the ratios of other activities or investments.

    B. The return on equity ratio is: net income for a period divided by beginning owner's equity.

    C. For proprietorships and partnerships, the formula can be modified to reflect the managerial services of the owners or partners by deducting the fair value of their efforts from net income.

Problem I

The following statements are either true or false. Place a (T) in the parentheses before each true statement and an (F) before each false statement.

1. ( ) The return on equity ratio is calculated by dividing owner's equity by net income.

2. ( ) An owner of a single proprietorship may have to sell all of his personal assets to satisfy the debts of his business, even if this amount exceeds the owner's equity in the business.

3. ( ) Land appraised at $40,000 and worth that much to its purchaser should be recorded at its worth ($40,000), even though it was purchased through hard bargaining for $35,000.

4. ( ) The statement of cash flows shows a company's revenues, expenses, and net income or loss.

5. ( ) Net income + Owner investments – Owner withdrawals = The increase in owner's equity during the year.

Problem II

You are given several words, phrases, or numbers to choose from in completing each of the following statements or in answering the following questions. In each case select the one that best completes the statement, or answers the question, and place its letter in the answer space provided.

_____ 1. Financial statement information about Boom Company is as follows:

December 31, 19X1:
Assets	$42,000
Liabilities	17,000

December 31, 19X2:
Assets	47,000
Liabilities	14,800

During 19X2:
Net income	18,000
Owner investments	?
Owner withdrawals	10,800

The amount of owner investments during 19X2 is:

a. $ 7,200.
b. $14,400.
c. $25,000.
d. $ 0.
e. Some other amount.

_____ 2. The seven-member nonprofit board that currently has the authority to identify generally accepted accounting principles is the:

a. APB.
b. FASB.
c. FEI.
d. ASB.
e. AICPA.

3. The business entity principle:

   a. States that revenue should be recognized at the time it is earned; the inflow of assets associated with revenue may be in a form other than cash; and the amount of revenue should be measured as the cash plus the cash equivalent value of any noncash assets received from customers in exchange for goods or services.
   b. Requires financial statements to reflect the assumption that the business will continue operating instead of being closed or sold, unless evidence shows that it will not continue.
   c. States that every business should be accounted for separately and distinctly from its owner or owners.
   d. Requires the financial statements to present information based on costs incurred in business transactions; it requires assets and services to be recorded initially at the cash or cash-equivalent amount given in exchange.
   e. Is another name for the going-concern principle.

4. Properties or economic resources owned by a business, or probable future economic benefits obtained or controlled by a particular entity as a result of past transactions or events, are called:

   a. Dividends.
   b. Assets.
   c. Retained earnings.
   d. Revenues.
   e. Owner's equity.

5. If on January 16, 19X1, Kay Bee Company rendered services for a customer in exchange for $175 cash, what would be the effects on the accounting equation?

   a. Assets, $175 increase; Liabilities, no effect; Owner's Equity, $175 increase.
   b. Assets, no effect; Liabilities, $175 decrease; Owner's Equity, $175 increase.
   c. Assets, $175 increase; Liabilities, $175 increase; Owner's Equity, no effect.
   d. Assets, $175 increase; Liabilities, $175 decrease; Owner's Equity, $350 increase.
   e. There is no effect on the accounting equation.

Problem III

Many of the important ideas and concepts discussed in Chapter 1 are reflected in the following list of key terms. Test your understanding of these terms by matching the appropriate definitions with the terms. Record the number identifying the most appropriate definition in the blank space next to each term.

____ AAA

____ Accounting equation

____ Accounts payable

____ Accounts receivable

____ AIMR

____ APB

____ ASB

____ Assets

____ Balance sheet

____ Balance sheet equation

____ Business entity principle

____ Business transaction

____ CAP

____ Common stock

____ Continuing-concern principle

____ Contributed capital

____ Corporation

____ Cost principle

____ Creditors

____ Debtors

____ Dividends

____ Equity

____ Expenses

____ FASB

____ FEI

____ GAAS

____ Generally accepted auditing standards

____ Going-concern principle

____ IASC

____ IMA

____ Income statement

____ Liabilities

____ Net assets

____ Net income

____ Net loss

____ Objectivity principle

____ Paid-in capital

____ Partnership

____ Realization principle

____ Retained earnings

____ Return on equity ratio

____ Revenue recognition principle

____ Revenues

____ Shareholders

____ SIA

____ Single proprietorship

____ Sole proprietorship

____ Statement of cash flows

____ Statement of changes in owner's equity

____ Statement of financial position

____ Statements of Financial Accounting Standards (SFAS)

____ Stock

____ Stockholders

____ Withdrawal

1. A financial statement providing information that helps users understand a company's financial status; lists the types and dollar amounts of assets, liabilities, and equity as of a specific date.

2. The accounting guideline that requires financial statement information to be supported by evidence other than someone's opinion or imagination adds to the reliability and usefulness of accounting information.

3. The name given to a corporation's stock when it issues only one kind or class of stock.

4. The category of stockholders' equity created by the stockholders' investments.

5. Payments of cash by a corporation to its stockholders.

6. Inflows of assets received in exchange for goods or services provided to customers as part of the major or central operations of the business; may occur as inflows of assets or decreases in liabilities.

7. The financial statement that shows whether the business earned a profit; it lists the types and amounts of the revenues and expenses.

8. Another name for the accounting equation.

9. A business chartered or incorporated as a separate legal entity under state or federal laws.

10. The accounting principle that requires financial statement information to be based on costs incurred in business transactions; it requires assets and services to be recorded initially at the cash or cash-equivalent amount given in exchange.

11. The difference between a company's assets and its liabilities; more precisely, the residual interest in the assets of an entity that remains after deducting its liabilities.

12. Financial Accounting Standards Board, the seven-member nonprofit board that currently has the authority to identify generally accepted accounting principles.

13. A business that is owned by two or more people and that is not organized as a corporation.

14. Another name for the balance sheet.

15. Another name for the revenue recognition principle.

16. Another name for contributed capital.

17. The excess of revenues over expenses for a period.

18. The category of stockholders' equity created by a corporation's profitable activities.

19. The rule that requires financial statements to reflect the assumption that the business will continue operating instead of being closed or sold, unless evidence shows that it will not continue.

20. The excess of expenses over revenues for a period.

21. Individuals or organizations that owe amounts to a business.

22. Outflows or the using up of assets as a result of the major or central operations of a business; also, liabilities may be increased.

23. The owners of a corporation.

24. Another name for a single proprietorship.

25. Assets created by selling goods and services on credit.

26. The rule that: (1) requires revenue to be recognized at the time it is earned, (2) allows the inflow of assets associated with revenue to be in a form other than cash, and (3) measures the amount of revenue as the cash plus the cash equivalent value of any noncash assets received from customers in exchange for goods or services.

27. An exchange between two parties of economic consideration, such as goods, services, money, or rights to collect money.

28. Equity of a corporation divided into units called shares.

29. A financial statement that shows the beginning balance of owner's equity, the changes in equity that resulted from new investments by the owner, net income (or net loss), and withdrawals, and the ending balance.

30. Individuals or organizations entitled to receive payments from a company.

31. Debts owed by a business or organization; probable future sacrifices of economic benefits arising from present obligations of a particular entity to transfer assets or provide services to other entities in the future as a result of past transactions or events.

32. The American Accounting Association, a professional association of college and university accounting faculty.

33. Another name for the going-concern principle.

34. Liabilities created by buying goods and services on credit.

35. Properties or economic resources owned by the business; more precisely, probable future economic benefits obtained or controlled by a particular entity as a result of past transactions or events.

36. The principle that requires every business to be accounted for separately and distinctly from its owner or owners; based on the goal of providing relevant information about the business.

37. A description of the relationship between a company's assets, liabilities, and equity; expressed as Assets = Liabilities + Owner's Equity.

38. Financial Executives Institute, a professional association of private accountants.

39. A business owned by one individual that is not organized as a corporation.

40. Accounting Principles Board, a former authoritative committee of the AICPA that was responsible for identifying generally accepted accounting principles from 1959 to 1973; predecessor to the FASB.

41. Another name for stockholders.

42. Institute of Management Accountants, a professional association of private accountants, formerly called the National Association of Accountants.

43. A financial statement that describes where a company's cash came from and where it went during the period; the cash flows are classified as being caused by operating, investing, and financing activities.

44. The publications of the FASB that establish new generally accepted accounting principles in the United States.

45. Another name for equity.

46. The Auditing Standards Board; the authoritative committee of the AICPA that identifies generally accepted auditing standards.

47. The Committee on Accounting Procedure; the authoritative body for identifying generally accepted accounting principles from 1936 to 1959.

48. International Accounting Standards Committee; a committee that attempts to create more harmony among the accounting practices of different countries by identifying preferred practices and encouraging their worldwide acceptance.

49. The abbreviation for generally accepted auditing standards.

50. Rules adopted by the accounting profession as guides for conducting audits of financial statements.

51. Securities Industry Association; an association of individuals involved with issuing and marketing securities.

52. Association for Investment Management and Research; a professional association of people who use financial statements in the process of evaluating companies' financial performance.

53. The ratio of net income to beginning owner's equity; used to judge a business's success compared to other activities or investments; may be modified for proprietorships or partnerships by subtracting the value of the owner's efforts in managing the business from the reported income.

54. A payment from a proprietorship or partnership to its owner or owners.

Problem IV

Complete the following by filling in the blanks.

1. The cost principle requires financial statement information to be based on _____ incurred in business transactions. The _____ principle requires financial statements to reflect the assumption that the business will continue operating instead of being closed or sold. The _____ principle requires financial statement information to be supported by evidence other than someone's opinion or imagination.

2. The _____ is a form of business organization that requires the organizers to obtain a charter from one of the states or the federal government.

3. Under the _____ principle, every business is to be accounted for as a separate entity, separate and distinct from its _____ or _____.

4. Assets created by selling goods and services on credit are called _____. Liabilities created by buying goods and services on credit are called _____.

5. Equity on a balance sheet is the difference between a company's _____ and its _____.

6. The statement of changes in owner's equity discloses all changes in equity during the period, including _____, _____, and _____.

7. The balance sheet equation is _____ equals _____ plus _____. It is also called the _____ equation.

8. Probable future sacrifices of economic benefits arising from present obligations of a particular entity to transfer assets or provide services to other entities in the future as a result of past transactions or events are called _____.

9. An excess of revenues over expenses for a period results in a _____. An excess of expenses over revenues results in a _____. The financial statement that lists revenues and expenses is the _____.

10. A balance sheet prepared for a business shows its financial position as of a specific _____. Financial position is shown by listing the _____ of the business, its _____, and its _____.

11. Expenses are outflows or the _____ of assets as a result of the major or central operations of a business.

12. The name given to a corporation's stock when it issues only one kind or class of stock is _____.

13. Individuals or organizations entitled to receive payments from a company are called _____. Individuals or organizations that owe amounts to a business are called _____.

14. The statement of cash flows shows the events that caused _____ to change. It classifies the cash flows into three major categories: _____, _____, and _____ activities.

Problem V

The assets, liabilities, and owner's equity of Linda Cornell's law practice are shown on the first line in the equation below, and following the equation are eight transactions completed by Ms. Cornell. Show by additions and subtractions in the spaces provided the effects of each transaction on the items of the equation. Show new totals after each transaction as in Illustration 1–7 in the text.

	Cash	+	Accounts Receivable	+	Prepaid Rent	+	Law Library	+	Office Equipment	=	Accounts Payable	+	L. Cornell, Capital
	$4,000						$12,000		$3,250				$19,250
1.													
2.													
3.													
4.													
5.													
6.													
7.													
8.													

(Column headings: ASSETS = LIABILITIES + OWNER'S EQUITY)

1. Paid the rent for three months in advance on the law office, $3,000.

2. Paid cash to purchase a new typewriter for the office, $900.

3. Completed legal work for Ray Holland and immediately collected the full payment of $2,500 in cash.

4. Purchased law books on credit, $700.

5. Completed $1,500 of legal work for Julie Landon on credit, and immediately entered in the accounting records both the right to collect and the revenue earned.

6. Paid for the law books purchased in Transaction 4.

7. Received $1,500 from Julie Landon for the legal work in Transaction 5.

8. Paid the weekly salary of the office secretary, $575.

Refer to your completed equation and fill in the blanks:

a. Did each transaction affect two items of the equation? _____
(Yes or No)

b. Did the equation remain in balance after the effects of each transaction were entered? _____
(Yes or No)

c. If the equation had not remained in balance after the effects of each transaction were entered, this would have indicated that _____ .

d. Ms. Cornell earned $2,500 of revenue upon the completion of Transaction 3, and the asset that flowed into the business as a result of this transaction was in the form of _____ .

e. Ms. Cornell earned $1,500 of revenue upon the completion of Transaction 5, and the asset that flowed into the business upon the completion of this transaction was _____ .

f. The right to collect $1,500 from Julie Landon was converted into _____ in Transaction 7. Nevertheless, the revenue was earned upon the completion of the _____ in Transaction 5.

g. The $1,500 collected in Transaction 7 was recognized as revenue in Transaction 5 because of the _____ principle, which states that (1) revenue should be recognized at the time it is _____ ; (2) the inflow of assets associated with revenue may be in a form other than _____ ; and (3) the amount of revenue should be measured as the cash plus the cash equivalent value of any _____ received from customers in exchange for goods or services.

Solutions for Chapter 1

Problem I

1. F
2. T
3. F
4. F
5. T

Problem II

1. D
2. B
3. C
4. B
5. A

Problem III

Problem IV

1. costs; going-concern; objectivity
2. corporation
3. business entity; owner; owners
4. accounts receivable; accounts payable
5. assets; liabilities
6. net income or net loss; new investments by the owner; withdrawals
7. Assets; Liabilities; Owner's Equity; accounting
8. liabilities
9. net income (profit); net loss; income statement
10. date; assets; liabilities; equity
11. using up (consuming)
12. common stock
13. creditors; debtors
14. cash; operating; investing; financing

Problem V

	Cash	+	Accounts Receivable	+	Prepaid Rent	+	Law Library	+	Office Equipment	=	Accounts Payable	+	L. Cornell, Capital
	$4,000						$12,000		$3,250				$19,250
1.	−3,000				+3,000								
	$1,000				$3,000		$12,000		$3,250					$19,250
2.	− 900								+ 900				
	$ 100				$3,000		$12,000		$4,150					$19,250
3.	+2,500													+ 2,500
	$2,600				$3,000		$12,000		$4,150					$21,750
4.							+ 700				+700			
	$2,600				$3,000		$12,700		$4,150		$700			$21,750
5.			+1,500											+ 1,500
	$2,600		$1,500		$3,000		$12,700		$4,150		$700			$23,250
6.	− 700										−700			
	$1,900		$1,500		$3,000		$12,700		$4,150		$ 0			$23,250
7.	+1,500		−1,500											
	$3,400		$ 0		$3,000		$12,700		$4,150		$ 0			$23,250
8.	− 575													− 575
	$2,825		$ 0		$3,000		$12,700		$4,150		$ 0			$22,675

a. Yes
b. Yes
c. an error had been made
d. cash
e. an account receivable
f. cash; legal work
g. revenue recognition (or realization); earned; cash; noncash assets

2 Recording Transactions

Learning Objective 1:

Describe the events recorded in accounting systems and the importance of source documents and business papers in those systems.

Summary

Accounting systems record transactions and other events that affect a company's assets, liabilities, and equity. The other events include internal transactions that use up assets or external events that cause the company's assets or liabilities to change. Source documents describe information that is recorded with accounting entries.

Learning Objective 2:

Describe how accounts are used to record information about the effects of transactions, how code numbers are used to identify each account, and the meaning of the words *debit* and *credit*.

Summary

Accounts are the basic building blocks of accounting systems. In one sense, accounts are symbols of the company's assets, liabilities, owner's equity, revenues, and expenses. In another sense, accounts are special records used to store information about transactions. The ledger is the collection of accounts used by an organization. Each account is assigned an identification number based on a code that indicates what kind of account it is. Debits record increases in assets, withdrawals, and expenses. Credits record decreases in these same accounts. Credits also record increases in liabilities, the owner's capital account, and revenues, while debits record decreases in these accounts.

Learning Objective 3:

Describe how debits and credits are used to analyze transactions and record their effects in the accounts.

Summary

To understand how a transaction affects a business, first determine what accounts were increased or decreased. Every transaction affects at least two accounts, and the sum of the debits for each transaction equals the sum of the credits. As a result, the effects of business transactions never create an imbalance in the accounting equation (Assets = Liabilities + Owner's Equity).

Learning Objective 4:

Record transactions in a General Journal, describe balance column accounts, and post entries from the journal to the ledger.

Summary

Transactions are first recorded in a journal that provides a record of all their effects in one location. Second, each entry in the journal is posted to the accounts in the ledger. This process places information in the accounts that is used to produce the company's financial statements. Balance column accounts are widely used in accounting systems. These accounts include columns for debit entries, credit entries, and the balance after each entry.

Learning Objective 5:

Prepare a trial balance, explain its usefulness, and calculate a company's debt ratio.

Summary

A trial balance is a list of the accounts in the ledger that shows their debit and credit balances in separate columns. The trial balance is a convenient summary of the ledger's contents. It also reveals the existence of some kinds of errors if the sum of the debit account balances does not equal the sum of the credit account balances. A company's debt ratio is the ratio between its total liabilities and total assets. It provides information about the risk a company faces by using liabilities to finance its assets.

Learning Objective 6:

Define or explain the words and phrases listed in the chapter glossary.

Summary

See Problem V.

Topical Outline

I. The accounting process:

    A. Begins with business papers, or source documents, which contain information about economic events and transactions (internal, external, and others) that take place in a business.

    B. Involves analyzing a company's economic events and business transactions and recording their effects.

    C. Also includes classifying and summarizing the recorded effects in reports or financial statements, which individuals find useful in making economic decisions about the entity.

II. The accounts

    A. Accounts are the basic building blocks of accounting systems used to develop a company's financial statements. They are the symbols of the company's assets, liabilities, owner's equity, revenues, and expenses, and are used to store information about the effects of transactions.

    B. There should be a separate account for each item on the income statement and balance sheet. The major types of accounts are:

        1. Asset accounts, including Cash, Accounts Receivable, Notes Receivable, Prepaid Expenses, Supplies, Equipment, Buildings, and Land.

        2. Liability accounts, including Accounts Payable, Notes Payable, and Unearned Revenues.

        3. Owner's equity accounts, including Capital, Withdrawals, Revenues, and Expenses.

    C. The ledger, also known as the book of final entry, is the collection of all the accounts used by a business in recording its transactions. The chart of accounts is a list of all the accounts.

III. Debits and credits

    A. A T-account is a simple account form used in accounting education to illustrate how debits and credits work.

        1. The left side of a T-account is called the debit side. A debit is an entry that increases asset and expense accounts, or decreases liability, owner's equity, and revenue accounts.

        2. The right side of a T-account is called the credit side. A credit is an entry that decreases asset and expense accounts, or increases liability, owner's equity, and revenue accounts.

        3. The account balance is the difference between the increases (including the beginning balance) and decreases recorded in an account.

    B. Double-entry accounting is an accounting system that records the effects of transactions and other events in at least two accounts with equal debits and credits. The total amount debited must equal the total amount credited. Therefore, the sum of the debit account balances in the ledger must equal the sum of the credit account balances.

IV. The journal (book of original entry)

    A. To help avoid errors, accounting systems first record transactions in a journal. The process of recording the transactions in a journal is called journalizing.

    B. A General Journal is the most flexible type of journal because it can be used to record any type of transaction. When a transaction is recorded in the General Journal, it is called a journal entry. A journal entry that affects more than two accounts is called a compound journal entry.

    C. Posting is the process of copying journal entry information from the journal to the accounts in the ledger. Actual accounting systems use balance column accounts rather than T-accounts in the ledger. A balance column account has debit and credit columns for recording entries and a third column for showing the balance of the account after each entry is posted.

V. The trial balance

A. A trial balance is a summary of the ledger that lists the accounts and their balances. The total debit balances should equal the total credit balances.

B. One purpose for preparing a trial balance is to test for the equality of the debit and credit account balances. Another reason is to simplify the task of preparing the financial statements.

C. When a trial balance does not balance (the columns are not equal), it means at least one error has occurred somewhere in the accounting process: in preparing the journal entries, posting the journal entries to the ledger, calculating account balances, copying account balances to the trial balance, or in totaling the trial balance columns. Any errors must be located and corrected before preparing the financial statements.

VI. The debt ratio:

A. Is the relationship between a company's liabilities and assets. It is calculated as: total liabilities divided by total assets.

B. Is used to describe the risk associated with a company's debts. Its size provides information about the risk faced by owners and creditors, and may indicate whether the company might be capable of increasing its income by going further into debt.

Problem I

The following statements are either true or false. Place a (T) in the parentheses before each true statement and an (F) before each false statement.

1. ( ) Debits are used to record increases in assets, withdrawals, and expenses.

2. ( ) The process of recording transactions in a journal is called posting.

3. ( ) In double-entry accounting, all errors are avoided by being sure that debits and credits are equal when transactions are recorded.

4. ( ) The cost of renting an office during the current period is an expense; however, the cost of renting an office six periods in advance is an asset.

5. ( ) The debt ratio is used to assess a company's risk of failing to pay its debts when they are due.

Problem II

You are given several words, phrases, or numbers to choose from in completing each of the following statements or in answering the following questions. In each case select the one that best completes the statement or answers the question and place its letter in the answer space provided.

_____ 1. Hans Hammer's company had a capital balance of $12,300 on June 30 and $23,800 on July 31. Net income for the month of July was $14,000. How much did Hammer withdraw from the business during July?

     a. $22,100.
     b. $25,500.
     c. $ 2,500.
     d. $11,500.
     e. $ 0.

_____ 2. Which of the following transactions does not affect the owner's equity in a proprietorship?

     a. Investments by the owner.
     b. Withdrawals of cash by the owner.
     c. Cash receipts for revenues.
     d. Cash receipts for unearned revenues.
     e. Cash payments for expenses.

_____ 3. A ledger is:

     a. A book of original entry in which the effects of transactions are first recorded.
     b. The collection of all accounts used by a business.
     c. A book of original entry in which any type of transaction can be recorded.
     d. A book of special journals.
     e. An account with debit and credit columns and a third column for showing the balance of the account.

4. The following transactions occurred during the month of October:

   1) Paid $1,500 cash for store equipment.
   2) Paid $1,000 in partial payment for supplies purchased 30 days previously.
   3) Paid October's utility bill of $600.
   4) Paid $1,200 to owner of business for his personal use.
   5) Paid $1,400 salary of office employee for October.

   What was the total amount of expenses during October?

   a. $3,000.
   b. $4,500.
   c. $2,000.
   d. $3,500.
   e. $5,700.

5. The journal entry to record the completion of legal work for a client on credit and billing the client $1,700 for the services rendered would be:

   a. Accounts Receivable 1,700
         Unearned Legal Fees 1,700
   b. Legal Fees Earned 1,700
         Accounts Receivable 1,700
   c. Accounts Payable 1,700
         Legal Fees Earned 1,700
   d. Legal Fees Earned 1,700
         Sales 1,700
   e. Accounts Receivable 1,700
         Legal Fees Earned 1,700

Problem III

Following are the first ten transactions completed by P. L. Wheeler's new business called Wheeler's Repair Shop:

a. Started the business with a cash deposit of $1,800 to a bank account in the name of the business.
b. Paid three months' rent in advance on the shop space, $675.
c. Purchased repair equipment for cash, $700.
d. Completed repair work for customers and collected cash, $1,005.50.
e. Purchased additional repair equipment on credit from Comet Company, $415.50.
f. Completed repair work on credit for Fred Baca, $175.
g. Paid Comet Company $290.50 of the amount owed from transaction (e).
h. Paid the local radio station $75 for an announcement of the shop opening.
i. Fred Baca paid for the work completed in transaction (f).
j. Withdrew $350 cash from the bank for P. L. Wheeler to pay personal expenses.

Required:

1. Record the transactions directly in the T-accounts that follow. Use the transaction letters to identify the amounts in the accounts.
2. Prepare a trial balance as of the current date using the form that follows.

Cash	Accounts Payable

	P. L. Wheeler, Capital

Accounts Receivable	P. L. Wheeler, Withdrawals

Prepaid Rent	Repair Services Revenue

Repair Equipment	Advertising Expense

Trial Balance

_____, 19_____

Problem IV

Journalize the following transactions and post to the accounts that follow.

a. On November 5 of the current year, Sherry Dale invested $1,500 in cash, and office equipment having a fair value of $950, to start a real estate agency.

b. On November 6, the business purchased office equipment for $425 cash.

GENERAL JOURNAL

DATE	ACCOUNT TITLES AND EXPLANATION	P.R.	DEBIT	CREDIT

Cash   Account No. 101

DATE	EXPLANATION	P.R.	DEBIT	CREDIT	BALANCE

Office Equipment   Account No. 163

DATE	EXPLANATION	P.R.	DEBIT	CREDIT	BALANCE

Sherry Dale, Capital   Account No. 301

DATE	EXPLANATION	P.R.	DEBIT	CREDIT	BALANCE

Problem V

Many of the important ideas and concepts discussed in Chapter 2 are reflected in the following list of key terms. Test your understanding of these terms by matching the appropriate definition with the terms. Record the number identifying the most appropriate definition in the blank space next to each term.

_____ Account   _____ General Journal

_____ Account balance   _____ Internal transactions

_____ Balance column account   _____ Journal

_____ Book of final entry   _____ Ledger

_____ Book of original entry   _____ Posting

_____ Business papers   _____ Posting Reference (PR) column

_____ Chart of accounts   _____ Prepaid expenses

_____ Compound journal entry   _____ Promissory note

_____ Credit   _____ Source documents

_____ Debit   _____ T-account

_____ Debt ratio   _____ Trial balance

_____ Double-entry accounting   _____ Unearned revenues

_____ External transactions

1. Liabilities created by advance cash payments from customers for products or services; satisfied by delivering the products or services in the future.

2. A summary of the ledger that lists the accounts and their balances; the total debit balances should equal the total credit balances.

3. An account with debit and credit columns for recording entries and a third column for showing the balance of the account after each debit or credit is posted.

4. Another name for business papers; the source of information recorded with accounting entries.

5. A record in which the effects of transactions are first recorded and from which amounts are posted to the ledger.

6. A place or location within an accounting system in which the increases and decreases in a specific asset, liability, owner's equity, revenue, or expense are recorded and stored.

7. A simple account form widely used in accounting education to illustrate how debits and credits work.

8. Various kinds of documents and other papers that companies use when they conduct their business.

9. An entry that increases asset and expense accounts, or decreases liability, owner's equity, and revenue accounts; recorded on the left side of a T-account.

10. Assets created by payments for economic benefits that are not used until later; then, as the benefits are used up, the cost of the assets becomes an expense.

11. The difference between the increases (including the beginning balance) and decreases recorded in an account.

12. A list of all accounts used by a company, including the identification number assigned to each account.

13. A journal entry that affects at least three accounts.

14. The most flexible type of journal; can be used to record any kind of transaction.

15. Another name for a journal.

16. Another name for a ledger.

17. An entry that decreases asset and expense accounts, or increases liability, owner's equity, and revenue accounts; recorded on the right side of a T-account.

18. An unconditional written promise to pay a definite sum of money on demand or on a defined future date (or dates).

19. The collection of all accounts used by a business.

20. The process of copying journal entry information to the ledger.

21. A term occasionally used to describe economic events that affect an entity's accounting equation but are not transactions between two parties.

22. An accounting system that records the effects of transactions and other events in at least two accounts with equal debits and credits.

23. A column in journals and accounts used to cross-reference journal and ledger entries.

24. Exchanges between the entity and some other person or organization.

25. The ratio between a company's liabilities and assets; used to describe the risk associated with the company's debts.

Problem VI

Complete the following by filling in the blanks.

1. The objectivity principle creates the need for credible _____, such as sales tickets, invoices, checks, bank statements, bills to customers, and employee earnings records.

2. The _____ is known as the book of original entry, while the _____ is known as the book of final entry.

3. The process of recording transactions in a journal is called _____. The process of transferring journal entry information to the ledger is called _____.

4. The _____ creates a link between a journal entry and the ledger accounts by providing a cross-reference for tracing the entry from one record to the other.

5. Notes receivable and prepaid insurance are examples of a(n) _____ account. Unearned revenues and interest payable are examples of a(n) _____ account.

6. Balances of _____ and _____ accounts flow into the income statement. Then, net income from the income statement and balances from _____ and _____ accounts flow into the statement of changes in owner's equity. Then, ending owner's equity and balances from _____ and _____ accounts flow into the balance sheet.

7. a. The normal balance of an asset account is a _____.

   b. The normal balance of a liability account is a _____.

   c. The normal balance of the capital account is a _____.

   d. The normal balance of the withdrawals account is a _____.

   e. The normal balance of a revenue account is a _____.

   f. The normal balance of an expense account is a _____.

8. When an account has the opposite of a normal balance, this abnormal balance can be indicated by

   _____.

9. The steps in preparing a trial balance are: _____

   _____

   _____

   _____

   _____

   _____

   _____

   _____

   _____

10. A trial balance that fails to balance is proof that _____
    either in journalizing, in posting, or in preparing the trial balance.

11. A trial balance that balances is not absolute proof that no errors were made because

    _____.

12. One frequent error that is made is called a _____, which occurs when two digits
    within a number are switched. This type of error probably has occurred if the difference between the two

    trial balance columns is evenly divisible by _____.

Solutions for Chapter 2

Problem I

1. T
2. F
3. F
4. T
5. T

Problem II

1. C
2. D
3. B
4. C
5. E

Problem III

	Cash				Repair Equipment			P. L. Wheeler, Withdrawals	
(a)	1,800.00	(b)	675.00	(c)	700.00		(j)	350.00	
(d)	1,005.50	(c)	700.00	(e)	415.50				
(i)	175.00	(g)	290.50						
		(h)	75.00						
		(j)	350.00						

	Accounts Receivable				Accounts Payable				Repair Services Revenue	
(f)	175.00	(i)	175.00	(g)	290.50	(e)	415.50	(d)	1,005.50	
								(f)	175.00	

	Prepaid Rent		P. L. Wheeler, Capital			Advertising Expense	
(b)	675.00		(a)	1,800.00	(h)	75.00	

WHEELER'S REPAIR SHOP
Trial Balance
(Current Date)

Cash	$ 890.00	
Prepaid rent	675.00	
Repair equipment	1,115.50	
Accounts payable		$ 125.00
P.L. Wheeler, capital		1,800.00
P.L. Wheeler, withdrawals	350.00	
Repair services revenue		1,180.50
Advertising expense	75.00	
Totals	$3,105.50	$3,105.50

Problem IV

GENERAL JOURNAL

Page 1

DATE	ACCOUNT TITLES AND EXPLANATION	P.R.	DEBIT	CREDIT
19— Nov. 5	Cash	101	1 500 00	
	Office Equipment	163	950 00	
	Sherry Dale, Capital	301		2 450 00
	Owner's initial investment.			
6	Office Equipment	163	425 00	
	Cash	101		425 00
	Purchased office equipment.			

GENERAL LEDGER

Cash
Account No. 101

DATE	EXPLANATION	P.R.	DEBIT	CREDIT	BALANCE
19— Nov. 5		G-1	1 500 00		1 500 00
6		G-1		425 00	1 075 00

Office Equipment
Account No. 163

DATE	EXPLANATION	P.R.	DEBIT	CREDIT	BALANCE
19— Nov. 5		G-1	950 00		950 00
6		G-1	425 00		1 375 00

Sherry Dale, Capital
Account No. 301

DATE	EXPLANATION	P.R.	DEBIT	CREDIT	BALANCE
19— Nov. 5		G-1		2 450 00	2 450 00

Problem V

Problem VI

1. source documents or business papers

2. journal, ledger

3. journalizing, posting

4. Posting Reference (PR) column

5. asset, liability

6. revenue, expense; capital, withdrawals; asset, liability

7. (a) debit; (b) credit; (c) credit; (d) debit; (e) credit; (f) debit

8. circling the amount or entering it in red

9. (1) Determine the balance of each account; (2) List in their ledger order the accounts having balances, with the debit balances in one column and the credit balances in another; (3) Add the debit balances; (4) Add the credit balances; (5) Compare the two totals for equality.

10. at least one error has been made

11. some types of errors do not create unequal debits and credits

12. transposition, nine

3 Adjusting the Accounts and Preparing the Statements

Learning Objective 1:

Explain why financial statements are prepared at the end of regular accounting periods, why the accounts must be adjusted at the end of each period, and why the accrual basis of accounting produces more useful income statements and balance sheets than the cash basis.

Summary

Companies prepare reports once each year. They also prepare interim financial statements because decision makers need information frequently and promptly. Adjusting entries are needed to capture information about unrecorded events that are not external transactions. The revenue recognition principle requires adjustments to ensure that revenue is reported when it is earned. The matching principle requires adjustments to ensure that expenses are reported in the same period as the revenue that was earned as a result of the expenses.

Accrual accounting is preferred to cash basis accounting because accrual accounting reports the economic effects of events when they occur, not when the cash flows happen. In addition to accrual basis financial statements, however, GAAP require companies to report a statement of cash flows.

Learning Objective 2:

Prepare adjusting entries for prepaid expenses, depreciation, unearned revenues, accrued expenses, and accrued revenues.

Summary

Adjusting entries are used *(a)* to record expenses when prepaid expenses expire, *(b)* to record depreciation expense as the cost of using plant and equipment assets, *(c)* to record revenues when the company converts unearned revenues to earned revenues, *(d)* to accrue expenses and related liabilities, and *(e)* to accrue revenues and related assets.

Learning Objective 3:

Prepare a schedule that includes the unadjusted trial balance, the adjustments, and the adjusted trial balance; use the adjusted trial balance to prepare financial statements; and prepare entries to record cash receipts and cash disbursements related to accrued assets and liabilities.

Summary

The effects of adjustments can be shown in a six-column schedule that presents the unadjusted trial balance in the first two columns, the adjusting entries in the next two columns, and the adjusted trial balance in the final two columns. The adjusted trial balance shows all ledger accounts, including assets, liabilities, revenues, expenses, and owner's equity. As a result, it can be used to prepare the income statement, the statement of changes in owner's equity, and the balance sheet.

Payments of accrued expenses in the next accounting period are recorded with a debit to the accrued liability and may include another debit for any additional expense incurred since the beginning of the new period. When accrued revenues are collected, the entry credits the previously recorded asset (a receivable) and may include another credit for any additional revenue earned during the new period.

Learning Objective 4:

Define each asset and liability category for the balance sheet, prepare a classified balance sheet, and calculate the current ratio.

Summary

Classified balance sheets usually report four categories of assets: current assets, investments, plant and equipment, and intangible assets. The two categories of liabilities are current and long-term. Owner's equity for proprietorships and partners' equity for partnerships are reported by putting the capital account balances on the balance sheet. A corporation reports stockholders' equity as contributed capital and retained earnings. A company's current ratio describes its ability to pay its current liabilities out of its current assets. The value of the ratio equals the amount of the current assets divided by the current liabilities.

Learning Objective 5:

Define or explain the words and phrases listed in the chapter glossary.

Summary

See Problem III.

Learning Objective 6 (Appendix A):

Explain why some companies record prepaid and unearned items in income statement accounts and prepare adjusting entries when this procedure is used.

Summary

Because many prepaid expenses expire during the same period they are purchased, some companies choose to charge all prepaid expenses to expense accounts at the time they are purchased. When this is done, end-of-period adjusting entries are required to transfer any unexpired amounts from the expense accounts to appropriate asset accounts. Also, unearned revenues may be credited to revenue accounts at the time cash is received. If so, end-of-period adjusting entries are required to transfer any unearned amounts from the revenue accounts to appropriate unearned revenue accounts.

Topical Outline

I. Adjusting the accounting records at the end of an accounting period

   A. Time-period principle—identifying the activities of a business with specific time periods such as months, or three-month periods, or years so that periodic financial reports of the business can be prepared. The specific period a business adopts is its:

      1. Fiscal year—the 12 consecutive months selected as an organization's annual accounting period. This annual accounting period may be the:

         a. Calendar year—January 1 to December 31.

         b. Natural business year—a 12-month period that ends when a company's sales activities are at their lowest point.

   B. The adjustment process—recording appropriate adjusting entries and assigning to each accounting period that portion of a transaction's effect applicable to the period, based on:

      1. The revenue recognition principle—requires revenue to be reported on the income statement only when it is earned, not before and not after.

      2. The matching principle—requires expenses to be reported in the same period as the revenues earned as a result of the expenses.

   C. Bases of accounting are the:

      1. Cash basis—revenues and expenses are recognized when cash is received or paid; no adjustments are made for prepaid, unearned, and accrued items.

      2. Accrual basis—the adjustment process is used to recognize revenues when they are earned and to match expenses with revenues.

   D. Accounts that require adjustments are:

      1. Prepaid expenses—economic benefits that are paid for in advance of use. They remain assets until they are consumed in the operation of the business.

      2. Depreciation—the expense created by allocating the cost of plant and equipment to the periods in which they are used.

      3. Unearned revenues—liabilities created by the receipt of cash from customers in payment for products or services that have not yet been delivered to the customers.

      4. Accrued expenses—incurred but unpaid expenses that are recorded during the adjusting process.

      5. Accrued revenues—earned but uncollected revenues that are recorded during the adjusting process.

II. Preparing financial statements

    A. The adjusted trial balance—prepared after end-of-period adjustments to the accounts have been made.

    B. Classifying balance sheet items

        1. Current assets—cash or other assets that are reasonably expected to be sold, collected, or consumed within one year or within the normal operating cycle of the business, whichever is longer; cash, short-term investments, accounts receivable, notes receivable, merchandise inventory, prepaid expenses.

        2. Investments—long-term assets such as stocks, bonds, promissory notes, and land held for future expansion.

        3. Plant and equipment—tangible, long-lived assets that are used to produce or sell goods and services; equipment, buildings, land.

        4. Intangible assets—assets that are used to produce or sell goods and services that do not have a physical form; their value comes from the privileges or rights that are granted to or held by the owner; goodwill, patents, trademarks, franchises, copyrights.

        5. Current liabilities—obligations due to be paid or liquidated within one year or the operating cycle, whichever is longer; accounts payable, notes payable, wages payable, taxes payable, interest payable, unearned revenues, current portions of long-term liabilities.

        6. Long-term liabilities—obligations that are not due to be paid within one year or the operating cycle of the business; notes payable, bonds payable.

        7. Equity—presentation depends on whether business is organized as a single proprietorship, partnership, or corporation.

    C. Balance sheet format

        1. Account form—places the liabilities and owner's equity to the right of the assets.

        2. Report form—vertical format, places the assets above the liabilities and the owner's equity.

III. Current ratio

    A. A description of a company's ability to pay its short-term obligations.

    B. Calculated as: $\dfrac{\text{Current assets}}{\text{Current liabilities}}$

IV. Appendix A

    A. If prepayments of expenses are debited to expense accounts, end-of-period adjusting entries must be designed to transfer unused or unexpired amounts to prepaid expense accounts.

    B. If cash receipts of unearned revenues are credited to revenue accounts, end-of-period adjusting entries must be designed to transfer remaining unearned amounts to liability accounts.

Problem I

The following statements are either true or false. Place a (T) in the parentheses before each true statement and an (F) before each false statement.

1. ( ) The effect of a debit to an unearned revenue account and a corresponding credit to a revenue account is to transfer the earned portion of the fee from the liability account to the revenue account.

2. ( ) If the accountant failed to make the end-of-period adjustment to remove from the Unearned Fees account the amount of fees earned, the omission would cause an overstatement of assets.

3. ( ) The economic effect of a revenue generally occurs when it is earned, not when cash is received.

4. ( ) The equity section of a balance sheet is the same for a single proprietorship, a partnership, or a corporation.

5. ( ) Under the cash basis of accounting, revenues are recognized when they are earned and expenses are matched with revenues.

6. ( ) A dividend's effect on a corporation is similar to that of a withdrawal on a proprietorship.

Problem II

You are given several words, phrases, or numbers to choose from in completing each of the following statements or in answering the following questions. In each case select the one that best completes the statement or answers the question and place its letter in the answer space provided.

_____ 1. The average time between paying cash for employee salaries or merchandise and receiving cash from customers is the:

    a. accounting period of a business.
    b. fiscal year.
    c. time-period principle.
    d. operating cycle of a business.
    e. natural business year.

_____ 2. X Company has four employees who are each paid $40 per day for a five-day work week. The employees are paid every Friday. If the accounting period ends on Wednesday, X Company should make the following entry to accrue wages:

    a. Salaries Expense   800
          Salaries Payable   800
    b. Salaries Expense   800
          Cash   800
    c. Salaries Expense   480
          Salaries Payable   480
    d. Salaries Expense   320
          Salaries Payable   320
    e. No entry should be made until the salaries are actually paid.

_____ 3. Lori Teach owns a sole proprietorship. During April of 19X1, Lori's business received $250 cash in advance for future services. The following entry should be made when the money is received:

    a. Cash   250
          Accounts Receivable   250
    b. Accounts Receivable   250
          Unearned Revenue   250
    c. Cash   250
          Unearned Revenue   250
    d. Unearned Revenue   250
          Services Revenue   250
    e. No entry should be made until services are actually rendered.

_____ 4. B & B Corporation had $175,000 of common stock issued and outstanding during all of 19X1. It began the year with $50,000 of retained earnings, and it declared and paid $10,000 of cash dividends to its stockholders. B & B earned a $15,000 net income in 19X1 and invested $5,000 in G. I. Jane common stock. What is the retained earnings balance at the end of 19X1?

    a. $230,000.
    b. $ 45,000.
    c. $ 40,000.
    d. $ 50,000.
    e. $ 55,000.

_____ 5. The Epicure Restaurant prepares monthly financial statements. On January 31, the balance in the Supplies account was $1,600. During February, $2,960 of supplies were purchased and debited to Supplies Expense. What is the adjusting entry on February 28 to account for the supplies assuming a February 28 inventory showed that $1,300 of supplies were on hand?

a.	Supplies Expense	300	
	Supplies		300
b.	Supplies	300	
	Supplies Expense		300
c.	Supplies	3,260	
	Cash		3,260
d.	Supplies Expense	3,260	
	Supplies		3,260
e.	Some other entry.		

_____ 6. ABC Company's balance sheet shows the following:

Current assets	$195,000
Total assets	850,000
Current liabilities	113,500
Total liabilities	441,500
Stockholders' equity	408,500

Calculate ABC's current ratio.

    a. 1.7
    b. 1.9
    c. 2.1
    d. 1.5
    e. 5.8

Problem III

Many of the important ideas and concepts discussed in Chapter 3 are reflected in the following list of key terms. Test your understanding of these terms by matching the appropriate definitions with the terms. Record the number identifying the most appropriate definition in the blank space next to each term.

_____	Account form balance sheet	_____	Dividends
_____	Accounting period	_____	Fiscal year
_____	Accrual basis accounting	_____	Intangible assets
_____	Accrued expenses	_____	Interim financial reports
_____	Accrued revenues	_____	Long-term liabilities
_____	Adjusted trial balance	_____	Matching principle
_____	Adjusting entry	_____	Natural business year
_____	Cash basis accounting	_____	Operating cycle of a
_____	Classified balance sheet		business
_____	Common stock	_____	Plant and equipment
_____	Contra account	_____	Report form balance sheet
_____	Current assets	_____	Time-period principle
_____	Current liabilities	_____	Unadjusted trial balance
_____	Current ratio	_____	Unclassified balance sheet
_____	Depreciation		

1. Incurred but unpaid expenses that are recorded during the adjusting process; recorded with a debit to an expense and a credit to a liability.

2. A description of a company's ability to pay its short-term obligations; calculated by dividing current assets by current liabilities.

3. Obligations that are not due to be paid within one year or the operating cycle, whichever is longer.

4. A trial balance prepared after adjustments have been recorded.

5. Earned but uncollected revenues that are recorded during the adjusting process; recorded with a credit to a revenue and a debit to an expense.

6. A trial balance prepared before adjustments have been recorded.

7. A broad principle that requires identifying the activities of a business with specific time periods such as months, quarters, or years.

8. The 12 consecutive months (or 52 weeks) selected as an organization's annual accounting period.

9. The expense created by allocating the cost of plant and equipment to the periods in which they are used; represents the expense of using the assets.

10. Tangible long-lived assets used to produce goods or services.

11. A journal entry at the end of an accounting period that recognizes revenues earned or expenses incurred in that period while updating the related liability and asset accounts.

12. The broad principle that requires expenses to be reported in the same period as the revenues that were earned as a result of the expenses.

13. A 12-month period that ends when a company's sales activities are at their lowest point.

14. A balance sheet that places the assets above the liabilities and owner's equity.

15. The approach to preparing financial statements based on recognizing revenues when the cash is received and reporting expenses when the cash is paid; not generally accepted.

16. Cash or other assets that are reasonably expected to be sold, collected, or consumed within one year or within the normal operating cycle of the business, whichever is longer.

17. The most basic category of a corporation's stock; if the corporation issues only one class of stock, all of it is common.

18. A balance sheet that does not separate the assets and liabilities into categories.

19. Assets without a physical form that are used to produce or sell goods and services; their value comes from the privileges or rights that are granted to or held by the owner.

20. The approach to preparing financial statements based on recognizing revenues when they are earned and matching expenses to those revenues; the basis for generally accepted accounting principles.

21. The average time between paying cash for employee salaries or merchandise and receiving cash from customers.

22. An account the balance of which is subtracted from the balance of a related account so that more complete information than simply the net amount is provided.

23. The length of time covered by periodic financial statements and other reports.

24. A balance sheet that places the liabilities and owner's equity to the right of the assets.

25. A balance sheet that presents the assets and liabilities in relevant groups.

26. A distribution, generally a cash payment, made by a corporation to its stockholders; similar to a withdrawal for a proprietorship.

27. Obligations due to be paid or liquidated within one year or the operating cycle, whichever is longer.

28. Financial reports covering less than one year; usually based on one- or three-month periods.

Problem IV

On October 1 of the current year, Harold Lloyd began business as a public stenographer. During the month he completed the following transactions:

Oct. 1 Invested $3,000 in the business.
    1 Paid three months' rent in advance on the office space, $1,245.
    1 Purchased office equipment for cash, $925.50.
    2 Purchased on credit office equipment, $700, and office supplies, $75.50.
   31 Completed stenographic work during the month and collected cash, $1,725. (Combined into one entry to conserve space.)
   31 Withdrew $725 for personal living expenses.

After the foregoing entries were recorded in the journal and posted, the accounts of Harold Lloyd appeared as follows:

GENERAL LEDGER

Cash   Account No. 101

DATE	EXPLANATION	P.R.	DEBIT	CREDIT	BALANCE
Oct. 1		G-1	3 000 00		3 000 00
1		G-1		1 245 00	1 755 00
1		G-1		925 50	829 50
31		G-2	1 725 00		2 554 50
31		G-2		725 00	1 829 50

Office Supplies   Account No. 124

DATE	EXPLANATION	P.R.	DEBIT	CREDIT	BALANCE
Oct. 2		G-1	75 50		75 50

Prepaid Rent   Account No. 131

DATE	EXPLANATION	P.R.	DEBIT	CREDIT	BALANCE
Oct. 1		G-1	1 245 00		1 245 00

Office Equipment — Account No. 163

DATE	EXPLANATION	P.R.	DEBIT	CREDIT	BALANCE
Oct. 1		G-1	925 50		925 50
2		G-1	700 00		1 625 50

Accumulated Depreciation, Office Equipment — Account No. 164

DATE	EXPLANATION	P.R.	DEBIT	CREDIT	BALANCE

Accounts Payable — Account No. 201

DATE	EXPLANATION	P.R.	DEBIT	CREDIT	BALANCE
Oct. 2		G-1		775 50	775 50

Harold Lloyd, Capital — Account No. 301

DATE	EXPLANATION	P.R.	DEBIT	CREDIT	BALANCE
Oct. 1		G-1		3 000 00	3 000 00

Harold Lloyd, Withdrawals — Account No. 302

DATE	EXPLANATION	P.R.	DEBIT	CREDIT	BALANCE
Oct. 31		G-2	725 00		725 00

Stenographic Services Revenue — Account No. 403

DATE	EXPLANATION	P.R.	DEBIT	CREDIT	BALANCE
Oct. 31		G-2		1 725 00	1 725 00

Depreciation Expense, Office Equipment
Account No. 612

DATE	EXPLANATION	P.R.	DEBIT	CREDIT	BALANCE

Rent Expense
Account No. 640

DATE	EXPLANATION	P.R.	DEBIT	CREDIT	BALANCE

Office Supplies Expense
Account No. 650

DATE	EXPLANATION	P.R.	DEBIT	CREDIT	BALANCE

On October 31, Harold Lloyd decided to adjust his accounts and prepare a balance sheet and an income statement. His adjustments were:

a. One month's rent had expired.

b. An inventory of office supplies showed $40 of unused office supplies.

c. The office equipment had depreciated $35 during October.

Required:

1. Prepare and post general journal entries to record the adjustments.

2. After posting the adjusting entries, complete the adjusted trial balance.

3. From the adjusted trial balance complete the income statement, statement of changes in owner's equity, and balance sheet.

DATE	ACCOUNT TITLES AND EXPLANATION	P.R.	DEBIT	CREDIT

HAROLD LLOYD
Adjusted Trial Balance
October 31, 19—

Account	Debit	Credit
Cash		
Office supplies		
Prepaid rent		
Office equipment		
Accumulated depreciation, office equipment		
Accounts payable		
Harold Lloyd, capital		
Harold Lloyd, withdrawals		
Stenographic services revenue		
Depreciation expense, office equipment		
Rent expense		
Office supplies expense		
Totals		

HAROLD LLOYD
Income Statement
For Month Ended October 31, 19—

Revenue:		
Stenographic services revenue		
Operating expenses:		
Depreciation expense, office equipment		
Rent expense		
Office supplies expense		
Total operating expenses		
Net income		

HAROLD LLOYD

Statement of Changes in Owner's Equity

For Month Ended October 31, 19—

Harold Lloyd, capital, October 1, 19—																
October net income																
Less withdrawals																
Excess of income over withdrawals																
Harold Lloyd, capital, October 31, 19—																

HAROLD LLOYD

Balance Sheet

October 31, 19—

Assets																							
Current Assets:																							
Cash																							
Office supplies																							
Prepaid rent																							
Total current assets																							
Plant and Equipment:																							
Office equipment																							
Less accumulated depreciation																							
Total plant and equipment																							
Total assets																							
Liabilities																							
Current Liabilities:																							
Accounts payable																							
Total liabilities																							
Owner's Equity																							
Harold Lloyd, capital, October 31, 19—																							
Total liabilities and owner's equity																							

Problem V

a. Blade Company has one employee who earns $72.50 per day. The company operates with monthly accounting periods, and the employee is paid each Friday night for a workweek that begins on Monday. Assume the calendar for October appears as shown and enter the four $362.50 weekly wage payments directly in the T-accounts below. Then enter the adjustment for the wages earned but unpaid on October 31.

OCTOBER						
S	M	T	W	T	F	S
	1	2	3	4	5	6
7	8	9	10	11	12	13
14	15	16	17	18	19	20
21	22	23	24	25	26	27
28	29	30	31			

Cash	Wages Payable	Wages Expense

b. Blade Company's October income statement should show $_____ of wages expense, and its October 31 balance sheet should show a $_____ liability for wages payable. The wages earned by its employee but unpaid on October 31 are an example of an _____ expense.

c. In the space that follows give the general journal entry to record payment of a full week's wages to the Blade Company employee on November 2.

GENERAL JOURNAL   Page 1

DATE	ACCOUNT TITLES AND EXPLANATION	P.R.	DEBIT	CREDIT

Problem VI

Riverview Properties operates an apartment building. On December 31, at the end of an annual accounting period, its Rent Earned account had a $335,500 credit balance, and the Unearned Rent account had a $3,600 credit balance. The following information was available for the year-end adjustments: (a) the credit balance in the Unearned Rent account resulted from a tenant paying his rent for six months in advance beginning on November 1; (b) also, a tenant in temporary financial difficulties had not paid his rent for the month of December. The amount due was $475.

Required: Enter the necessary adjustments directly in the T-accounts below.

Rent Receivable	Unearned Rent	Rent Earned
	Nov. 1 3,600	Bal. 335,500

After the foregoing adjustments are entered in the accounts, the company's Rent Earned account has a $_____ balance which should appear on its income statement as revenue earned during the year. Its Unearned Rent account has a $_____ balance, and this should appear on the company's balance sheet as a _____ . Likewise, the company's Rent Receivable account has a $_____ balance, and this should appear on its balance sheet as a _____ .

Problem VII

1. Under the cash basis of accounting, revenues are reported as being earned in the accounting period in which _____ ; expenses are charged to the period in which _____ ; and net income for the period is the difference between _____ and _____ . Under the accrual basis of accounting, revenues are credited to the period in which _____ , expenses are _____ with revenues, and no consideration is given as to when cash is received or disbursed.

2. Current assets consist of cash or other assets that are reasonably expected to be (complete definition) _____
_____
_____
_____
_____ .

Problem VIII (This problem applies to Appendix A.)

The following statements are either true or false. Place a (T) in the parentheses before each true statement and an (F) before each false statement.

1. (   ) If a business follows the practice of debiting prepayments of expenses to expense accounts, the adjusting entries for prepaid expenses require debits to prepaid expense accounts.

2. (   ) If a business records receipts of unearned revenues with debits to cash and credits to revenue accounts, no adjusting entries are required at the end of the period.

Problem IX (This problem applies to Appendix A.)

You are given several words, phrases, or numbers to choose from in completing each of the following statements or in answering the following questions. In each case select the one that best completes the statement or answers the question and place its letter in the answer space provided.

_____ 1. Hanover Company prepares monthly financial statements and follows the procedure of crediting revenue accounts when it records cash receipts of unearned revenues. During April, the business received $4,800 for services to be rendered during April and May. On April 30, $2,000 of the amounts received had been earned. What is the adjusting journal entry on April 30 for service fees?

    a. Service Fees Earned 2,000
        Unearned Service Fees   2,000
    b. Unearned Service Fees 2,800
        Service Fees Earned   2,800
    c. Cash 2,000
        Service Fees Earned   2,000
    d. Unearned Service Fees 2,000
        Service Fees Earned   2,000
    e. Service Fees Earned 2,800
        Unearned Service Fees   2,800

_____ 2. Xanadu Company prepares monthly financial statements. On August 31, the balance in the Office Supplies account was $300. During September, $500 of supplies were purchased and debited to Office Supplies Expense. What is the adjusting journal entry on September 30 to account for the supplies assuming a September inventory of supplies showed that $250 were on hand.

    a. Office Supplies 350
        Office Supplies Expense   350
    b. Office Supplies Expense 250
        Office Supplies   250
    c. Office Supplies Expense 50
        Office Supplies   50
    d. Office Supplies Expense 350
        Office Supplies   350
    e. Office Supplies 250
        Office Supplies Expense   250

Solutions for Chapter 3

Problem I

1. T
2. F
3. T
4. F
5. F
6. T

Problem II

1. D
2. C
3. C
4. E
5. A
6. A

Problem III

Problem IV

Oct. 31	Rent Expense	415.00	
	Prepaid Rent		415.00
31	Office Supplies Expense	35.50	
	Office Supplies		35.50
31	Depreciation Expense, Office Equipment	35.00	
	Accumulated Depr., Office Equipment		35.00

Cash

Date		Debit	Credit	Balance
Oct.	1	3,000.00		3,000.00
	1		1,245.00	1,755.00
	1		925.50	829.50
	31	1,725.00		2,554.50
	31		725.00	1,829.50

Office Supplies

Date		Debit	Credit	Balance
Oct.	2	75.50		75.50
	31		35.50	40.00

Prepaid Rent

Date		Debit	Credit	Balance
Oct.	1	1,245.00		1,245.00
	31		415.00	830.00

Office Equipment

Date		Debit	Credit	Balance
Oct.	1	925.50		925.50
	2	700.00		1,625.50

Accumulated Depr., Office Equipment

Date		Debit	Credit	Balance
Oct.	31		35.00	35.00

Accounts Payable

Date		Debit	Credit	Balance
Oct.	2		775.50	775.50

Harold Lloyd, Capital

Date		Debit	Credit	Balance
Oct.	1		3,000.00	3,000.00

Harold Lloyd, Withdrawals

Date		Debit	Credit	Balance
Oct.	31	725.00		725.00

Stenographic Services Revenue

Date		Debit	Credit	Balance
Oct.	31		1,725.00	1,725.00

Depr. Expense, Office Equipment

Date		Debit	Credit	Balance
Oct.	31	35.00		35.00

Rent Expense

Date		Debit	Credit	Balance
Oct.	31	415.00		415.00

Office Supplies Expense

Date		Debit	Credit	Balance
Oct.	31	35.50		35.50

HAROLD LLOYD
Adjusted Trial Balance
October 31, 19--

	Debit	Credit
Cash	$1,829.50	
Office supplies	40.00	
Prepaid rent	830.00	
Office equipment	1,625.50	
Accumulated depreciation, office equipment		$ 35.00
Accounts payable		775.50
Harold Lloyd, capital		3,000.00
Harold Lloyd, withdrawals	725.00	
Stenographic services revenue		1,725.00
Depreciation expense, office equipment	35.00	
Rent expense	415.00	
Office supplies expense	35.50	
Totals	$5,535.50	$5,535.50

HAROLD LLOYD
Income Statement
For Month Ended October 31, 19--

Revenue:
Stenographic services revenue $1,725.00
Operating expenses:
Depreciation expense, office equipment .... $ 35.00
Rent expense 415.00
Office supplies expense 35.50
Total operating expenses 485.50
Net income $1,239.50

HAROLD LLOYD
Statement of Changes in Owner's Equity
For Month Ended October 31, 19--

Harold Lloyd, capital, October 1, 19-- $3,000.00
October net income $1,239.50
Less withdrawals 725.00
Excess of income over withdrawals 514.50
Harold Lloyd, capital, October 31, 19-- $3,514.50

HAROLD LLOYD
Balance Sheet
October 31, 19--

Assets

Current Assets:
Cash $1,829.50
Office supplies 40.00
Prepaid rent 830.00
Total current assets $2,699.50
Plant and Equipment:
Office equipment $1,625.50
Less accumulated depreciation 35.00
Total plant and equipment 1,590.50
Total assets $4,290.00

Liabilities

Current Liabilities:
Accounts payable .... $ 775.50
Total liabilities .... $ 775.50

Owner's Equity

Harold Lloyd, capital, October 31, 19-- 3,514.50
Total liabilities and owner's equity $4,290.00

Problem V

a.

	Cash				Wages Expense	
	Oct. 5	362.50		Oct. 5	362.50	
	12	362.50		12	362.50	
	19	362.50		19	362.50	
	26	362.50		26	362.50	
				31	217.50	

	Wages Payable	
	Oct. 31	217.50

b. $1,667.50; $217.50; accrued

c. Nov. 2   Wages Expense 145.00
              Wages Payable 217.50
                 Cash 362.50

Problem VI

	Rent Receivable				Unearned Rent		
Dec. 31	475			Dec. 31	1,200	Nov. 1	3,600

	Rent Earned	
	Bal.	335,500
	Dec. 31	1,200
	31	475

Rent Earned, $337,175
Unearned Rent, $2,400, current liability
Rent Receivable, $475, current asset

Problem VII

1. they are received in cash, they are paid, revenue receipts, expense disbursements, earned, matched

2. sold, collected, or consumed within one year or within the normal operating cycle of the business, whichever is longer.

Problem VIII

1. T
2. F

Problem IX

1. E
2. C

4   The Work Sheet and the Closing Process

Learning Objective 1:

Explain why work sheets are useful, prepare a work sheet for a service business, and prepare financial statements from the information in a work sheet.

Summary

Accountants often use work sheets at the end of an accounting period in the process of preparing adjusting entries, the adjusted trial balance, and the financial statements. The work sheet is only a tool for accountants and is not distributed to investors or creditors. The work sheet described in this chapter has five pairs of columns for the unadjusted trial balance, the adjustments, the adjusted trial balance, the income statement, and the statement of changes in owner's equity and the balance sheet. Other formats are used in practice.

The income statement is prepared from the Income Statement columns of the work sheet by taking the revenues from the Credit column and the expenses from the Debit column. The net income is the difference between the debits and credits. The statement of changes in owner's equity combines the pre-closing balance of the capital account (including the beginning balance plus any new investments), the net income from the Income Statement columns, and the owner's withdrawals. The balance sheet combines all assets, contra assets, and liabilities from the last two columns of the work sheet with the ending balance of owner's equity presented in the statement of changes in owner's equity.

Learning Objective 2:

Explain why the temporary accounts are closed at the end of each accounting period and prepare closing entries and a post-closing trial balance for a service business.

Summary

The temporary accounts are closed at the end of each accounting period for two reasons. First, this process prepares the revenue, expense, and withdrawals accounts for the next reporting period by giving them zero balances. Second, it updates the owner's equity account to include the effects of all economic events recorded for the year. The revenue and expense account balances are initially transferred to the Income Summary account, which is then closed to the owner's capital accounts. Finally, the withdrawals account is closed to the capital account.

Learning Objective 3:

Describe each step in the accounting cycle.

Summary

The accounting cycle consists of eight steps: (1) journalizing external transactions and (2) posting the entries during the year, and, at the end of the year: (3) preparing either an unadjusted trial balance or (4) a work sheet, (5) preparing and posting adjusting entries, (6) preparing the financial statements, (7) preparing and posting closing entries, and (8) preparing the post-closing trial balance.

Learning Objective 4:

Calculate the profit margin ratio and describe what it reveals about a company's performance.

Summary

The profit margin ratio describes a company's income earning activities by showing the period's net income as a percentage of total revenue. It is found by dividing the reporting period's net income by the revenue for the same period. The ratio can be usefully interpreted only in light of additional facts about the company and its industry.

Learning Objective 5:

Define or explain the words and phrases listed in the chapter glossary.

Summary

See Problem III.

Learning Objective 6 (Appendix B):

Explain when and why reversing entries are used and prepare reversing entries.

Summary

Optional reversing entries can be applied to accrued assets and liabilities, including accrued interest earned, accrued interest expense, accrued taxes, and accrued salaries or wages. The goal of reversing entries is to simplify subsequent journal entries. The financial statements are not affected by the choice. Reversing entries are used simply as a matter of convenience in bookkeeping.

Topical Outline

I. The work sheet and adjusting entries

    A. Preparing a work sheet is useful:

        1. In preparing financial statements.

        2. As an educational tool.

        3. For planning major transactions.

        4. For auditing purposes.

    B. To prepare a work sheet:

        1. List all accounts contained in the unadjusted trial balance.

        2. Enter the adjustments and combine with the unadjusted trial balance to prepare the adjusted trial balance. Total the Adjusted Trial Balance columns to ensure debits and credits equal.

        3. Extend adjusted trial balance amounts to the financial statement columns.

        4. Determine net income (or loss) by taking the difference between debit and credit totals of Income Statement columns, and balance the Statement of Changes in Owner's Equity and Balance Sheet columns by adding net income (or loss).

    C. Prepare the financial statements and journalize and post the adjusting entries.

II. Closing entries

    A. Closing entries are made to:

        1. Transfer the effects of revenues, expenses, and withdrawals to the capital account.

        2. Bring the temporary (revenue, expense, withdrawals, and Income Summary) account balances to zero, so that revenues, expenses, and withdrawals in the next accounting period can be properly recorded and closed.

    B. Closing the accounts

        1. Revenue accounts, which have credit balances, are closed by debiting the accounts and crediting Income Summary.

        2. Expense accounts, which have debit balances, are closed by crediting the accounts and debiting Income Summary.

        3. The balance of the Income Summary account is transferred to the proprietor's capital account. For corporations, the balance of the Income Summary account is transferred to Retained Earnings.

        4. The withdrawals account is closed by crediting the account and debiting the proprietor's capital account. (This step differs for corporations because withdrawals accounts are not used.)

    C. Accounts that appear in the balance sheet are called real or permanent accounts. Those that are closed at the end of each period are called nominal or temporary accounts.

III. The accounting cycle—the sequence of accounting procedures followed each accounting period:

    A. Journalizing

    B. Posting

    C. Preparing an unadjusted trial balance

    D. Completing the work sheet

    E. Adjusting the accounts

    F. Preparing the financial statements

    G. Closing the temporary accounts

    H. Preparing a post-closing trial balance

IV. Profit margin

    A. Measures the average proportion of each dollar of revenue that ends up as profit.

    B. Calculated as: $\dfrac{\text{Net income}}{\text{Revenues}}$

V. Appendix B: Reversing entries

    A. Reversing entries are optional entries prepared after closing entries and dated the first day of the new period.

    B. Reversing entries are usually applied to asset and liability account balances that arose from the accrual of revenues and expenses.

    C. The accrued asset and liability account balances are transferred to related revenue and expense accounts.

    D. When reversing entries are used, subsequent cash receipts (and payments) are recorded in revenue (and expense) accounts.

Problem I

The following statements are either true or false. Place a (T) in the parentheses before each true statement and an (F) before each false statement.

1. ( ) If the Income Statement columns of a work sheet are equal after transferring from the Adjusted Trial Balance columns, then it can be concluded that there is no net income (or loss).

2. ( ) The only reason why the Statement of Changes in Owner's Equity or Balance Sheet columns of a work sheet might be out of balance would be if an error had been made in sorting revenue and expense data from the Adjusted Trial Balance columns of the work sheet.

3. ( ) After all closing entries are posted at the end of an accounting period, the Income Summary account balance is zero.

4. ( ) Throughout the current period, one could refer to the balance of the Income Summary account to determine the amount of net income or loss that was earned in the prior accounting period.

5. ( ) On a work sheet, net income would be understated if a liability was extended into the Income Statement—Credit column.

Problem II

You are given several words, phrases, or numbers to choose from in completing each of the following statements or in answering the following questions. In each case select the one that best completes the statement or answers the question and place its letter in the answer space provided.

_____ 1. Equipment, Wages Expense, and The Owner, Capital would be sorted to which respective columns in completing a work sheet?

    a. Statement of Changes in Owner's Equity or Balance Sheet—Debit; Income Statement—Debit; and Statement of Changes in Owner's Equity or Balance Sheet—Debit.

    b. Statement of Changes in Owner's Equity or Balance Sheet—Debit; Income Statement—Debit; and Statement of Changes in Owner's Equity or Balance Sheet—Credit.

    c. Statement of Changes in Owner's Equity or Balance Sheet—Debit; Income Statement—Credit; and Statement of Changes in Owner's Equity or Balance Sheet—Debit.

    d. Statement of Changes in Owner's Equity or Balance Sheet—Debit; Income Statement—Credit; and Statement of Changes in Owner's Equity or Balance Sheet—Credit.

    e. Statement of Changes in Owner's Equity or Balance Sheet—Credit; Income Statement—Credit; and Statement of Changes in Owner's Equity or Balance Sheet—Credit.

_____ 2. Based on the following T-accounts and their end-of-period balances, what will be the balance of the Joe Cool, Capital account after the closing entries are posted?

Joe Cool, Capital		Joe Cool, Withdrawals		Income Summary	
	Dec. 31 7,000	Dec. 31 9,600			

Revenue		Rent Expense		Salaries Expense	
	Dec. 31 29,700	Dec. 31 3,600		Dec. 31 7,200	

Insurance Expense		Depr. Expense, Equipment		Accum. Depr., Equipment	
Dec. 31 920		Dec. 31 500			Dec. 31 500

  a. $12,880 Debit.
  b. $12,880 Credit.
  c. $24,480 Credit.
  d. $14,880 Credit.
  e. $10,480 Debit.

_____ 3. The following items appeared on a December 31 work sheet. Based on the following information, what are the totals in the Statement of Changes in Owner's Equity or Balance Sheet columns?

	Unadjusted Trial Balance		Adjustments	
	Debit	Credit	Debit	Credit
Cash	975			
Supplies	180			70
Prepaid insurance	3,600			150
Equipment	10,320			
Accounts payable		1,140		
Unearned fees		4,500	375	
The Owner, capital		9,180		
The Owner, withdrawals	1,650			
Fees earned		5,850		375
				300
Salaries expense	2,100		315	
Rent expense	1,500			
Utilities expense	345			
	20,670	20,670		
Insurance expense			150	
Supplies expense			70	
Depreciation expense, equipment			190	
Accumulated depreciation, equipment				190
Salaries payable				315
Accounts receivable			300	
			1,400	1,400

  a. $16,805.
  b. $16,505.
  c. $14,950.
  d. $14,820.
  e. Some other amount.

_____ 4. In what order are the following steps in the accounting cycle performed?

        1) Preparing an unadjusted trial balance
        2) Journalizing and posting closing entries
        3) Journalizing transactions
        4) Preparing a post-closing trial balance
        5) Preparing the financial statements
        6) Completing the work sheet
        7) Journalizing and posting adjusting entries
        8) Posting the entries to record transactions

    a. (1),(3),(8),(7),(6),(2),(4),(5)
    b. (3),(8),(1),(6),(5),(7),(2),(4)
    c. (1),(3),(8),(6),(7),(2),(5),(4)
    d. (3),(1),(8),(7),(6),(5),(4),(2)
    e. (3),(8),(1),(7),(6),(2),(4),(5)

_____ 5. Real accounts are:

    a. Accounts that are closed at the end of the accounting period; therefore, the revenue, expense, Income Summary, and withdrawals accounts.
    b. Accounts used to record the owner's investment in the business plus any more or less permanent changes in the owner's equity.
    c. Accounts the balance of which is subtracted from the balance of an associated account to show a more proper amount for the item recorded in the associated account.
    d. Also called temporary accounts.
    e. Also called permanent accounts.

_____ 6. The following information is available from the financial statements of Harvard Company:

Total assets	$475,200
Revenues	862,600
Gross profit	345,040
Net income	110,000

Harvard's profit margin is:

    a. 40.0%.
    b. 72.6%.
    c. 12.8%.
    d. 31.9%.
    e. 23.1%.

Problem III

Many of the important ideas and concepts discussed in Chapter 4 are reflected in the following list of key terms. Test your understanding of these terms by matching the appropriate definitions with the terms. Record the number identifying the most appropriate definition in the blank space next to each term.

_____ Accounting cycle

_____ Closing entries

_____ Income Summary

_____ Nominal accounts

_____ Permanent accounts

_____ Post-closing trial balance

_____ Profit margin

_____ Pro forma statements

_____ Real accounts

_____ Return on sales

_____ Reversing entries

_____ Temporary accounts

_____ Work sheet

_____ Working papers

1. The ratio of a company's net income to its revenues; measures the average proportion of each dollar of revenue that ends up as profit.

2. A trial balance prepared after the closing entries have been posted; the final step in the accounting cycle.

3. Eight recurring steps performed each accounting period, starting with recording transactions in the journal and continuing through the post-closing trial balance.

4. Another name for profit margin.

5. Accounts that are used to describe revenues, expenses, and owner's withdrawals; they are closed at the end of the reporting period.

6. Analyses and other informal reports prepared by accountants when organizing the useful information presented in formal reports to internal and external decision makers.

7. Accounts that are used to describe assets, liabilities, and owner's equity; they are not closed as long as the company continues to own the assets, owe the liabilities, or have owner's equity; the balances of these accounts appear on the balance sheet.

8. Another name for temporary accounts.

9. The special account used only in the closing process to temporarily hold the amounts of revenues and expenses before the net difference is added to (or subtracted from) the owner's capital account or the Retained Earnings account for a corporation.

10. Optional entries recorded at the beginning of a new year that prepare the accounts for simplified journal entries subsequent to accrual adjusting entries.

11. Journal entries recorded at the end of each accounting period to prepare the revenue, expense, and withdrawals accounts for the upcoming year and update the owner's capital account for the events of the year just finished.

12. A 10-column spreadsheet used to draft a company's unadjusted trial balance, adjusting entries, adjusted trial balance, and financial statements; an optional step in the accounting process.

13. Another name for permanent accounts.

14. Statements that show the effects of the proposed transactions as if the transactions had already occurred.

Problem IV

Complete the following by filling in the blanks.

1. A work sheet is prepared after all transactions are recorded but before _____ _____ .

2. Revenue accounts have credit balances; consequently, to close a revenue acccount and make it show a zero balance, the revenue account is _____ and the Income Summary account is _____ for the amount of the balance.

3. In extending the amounts in the Adjusted Trial Balance columns of a work sheet to the proper Income Statement or Statement of Changes in Owner's Equity and Balance Sheet columns, two decisions are involved. The decisions are:

   (a) _____ and

   (b) _____ .

4. Expense accounts have debit balances; therefore, expense accounts are _____ and the Income Summary account is _____ in closing the expense accounts.

5. In preparing a work sheet for a concern, its unadjusted account balances are entered in the _____ of the work sheet form, after which the _____ are entered in the second pair of columns. Next, the unadjusted trial balance amounts and the amounts in the Adjustments columns are combined to secure an _____ in the third pair of columns.

6. Only balance sheet accounts should have balances appearing on the post-closing trial balance because the balances of all temporary accounts are reduced to _____ in the closing procedure.

7. Closing entries are necessary because if at the end of an accounting period the revenue and expense accounts are to show only one period's revenues and expenses, they must begin the period with _____ balances, and closing entries cause the revenue and expense accounts to begin a new period with _____ balances.

8. Closing entries accomplish two purposes: (1) they cause all _____ accounts to begin the new accounting period with zero balances, and (2) they transfer the net effect of the past period's _____ , _____ , and withdrawal transactions to the owner's capital account.

9. The profit margin measures the percentage of _____ that ends up as profit.

Problem V

The unfinished year-end work sheet of Homer's Home Shop appears on the next page.

Required:

1. Complete the work sheet using the following adjustments information:

   a. A $725 inventory of shop supplies indicates that $1,037 of shop supplies have been used during the year.

   b. The shop equipment has depreciated $475 during the year.

   c. On December 31, wages of $388 have been earned by the one employee but are unpaid because payment is not due.

2. After completing the work sheet, prepare the year-end adjusting and closing entries.

3. Post the adjusting and closing entries to the accounts that appear in skeletonized form beginning on page 000.

4. After posting the adjusting and closing entries, prepare a post-closing trial balance.

HOMER'S HOME SHOP
Work Sheet for Year Ended December 31, 19—

Account	Unadjusted Trial Balance Dr.	Unadjusted Trial Balance Cr.	Adjustments Dr.	Adjustments Cr.	Adjusted Trial Balance Dr.	Adjusted Trial Balance Cr.	Income Statement Dr.	Income Statement Cr.	Stmt. of Ch. in O.E. and Balance Sheet Dr.	Stmt. of Ch. in O.E. and Balance Sheet Cr.
Cash	2 8 7 5 00									
Accounts receivable	2 0 0 0 00									
Shop supplies	1 7 6 2 00									
Shop equipment	5 1 2 5 00									
Accumulated depreciation, shop equipment		7 2 5 00								
Accounts payable		5 7 5 00								
Homer Tonely, capital		5 5 0 0 00								
Homer Tonely, withdrawals	30 0 0 0 00									
Repair services revenue		55 7 8 5 00								
Wages expense	18 2 5 0 00									
Rent expense	2 5 0 0 00									
Miscellaneous expenses	7 3 00									
	62 5 8 5 00	62 5 8 5 00								
Shop supplies expense										
Depreciation expense, shop equipment										
Wages payable										

DATE	ACCOUNT TITLES AND EXPLANATION	P.R.	DEBIT	CREDIT

GENERAL LEDGER

Cash

Date	Debit	Credit	Balance
Dec. 31			2,875.00

Accounts Receivable

Date	Debit	Credit	Balance
Dec. 31			2,000.00

Shop Supplies

Date	Debit	Credit	Balance
Dec. 31			1,762.00

Shop Equipment

Date	Debit	Credit	Balance
Dec. 31			5,125.00

Accum. Depr., Shop Equipment

Date	Debit	Credit	Balance
Dec. 31			725.00

Accounts Payable

Date	Debit	Credit	Balance
Dec. 31			575.00

Wages Payable

Date	Debit	Credit	Balance

Homer Tonely, Capital

Date	Debit	Credit	Balance
Dec. 31			5,500.00

Homer Tonely, Withdrawals

Date	Debit	Credit	Balance
Dec. 31			30,000.00

Repair Services Revenue

Date	Debit	Credit	Balance
Dec. 31			55,785.00

Depr. Expense, Shop Equipment

Date	Debit	Credit	Balance

Wages Expense

Date	Debit	Credit	Balance
Dec. 31			18,250.00

Rent Expense

Date	Debit	Credit	Balance
Dec. 31			2,500.00

Shop Supplies Expense

Date	Debit	Credit	Balance

Miscellaneous Expenses

Date	Debit	Credit	Balance
Dec. 31			73.00

Income Summary

Date	Debit	Credit	Balance

HOMER'S HOME SHOP

Post-Closing Trial Balance

December 31, 19—

Cash									
Accounts receivable									
Shop supplies									
Shop equipment									
Accumulated depreciation, shop equipment									
Accounts payable									
Wages payable									
Homer Tonely, capital									
Totals									

Problem VI (This problem applies to Appendix B.)

The following statements are either true or false. Place a (T) in the parentheses before each true statement and an (F) before each false statement.

1. ( )   After the adjusting, closing, and reversing entries are posted to an account where there were end-of-period adjustments of accrued items, the account will have an opposite from normal balance.

2. ( )   Reversing entries are used only for accruals of expense items such as Salaries Expense, Tax Expense, and Interest Expense.

3. ( )   Some companies initially record prepaid expenses with debits to expense accounts and then make end-of-period adjusting entries to transfer unexpired amounts to asset accounts. These companies may then use reversing entries to transfer the unexpired amounts back into expense accounts.

Problem VII (This problem applies to Appendix B.)

You are given several words, phrases, or numbers to choose from in completing each of the following statements or in answering the following questions. In each case select the one that best completes the statement or answers the question and place its letter in the answer space provided.

_____ 1. The December 31, 19X1, adjusting entries for Mary Swan's interior design company included accrual of $760 in secretarial salaries. This amount will be paid on January 5, as part of the normal $1,200 salary for two weeks. The bookkeeper for the company uses reversing entries where appropriate. When the secretary's salary was paid on January 10, 19X2, the following entry was made:

| Jan. 10 | Salaries Expense | 1,200 | |
| | Cash | | 1,200 |

What was the January 1, 19X2, reversing entry?

a.	Salaries Payable	760	
	Salaries Expense	440	
	Cash		1,200
b.	Salaries Payable	440	
	Salaries Expense		440
c.	Salaries Payable	760	
	Salaries Expense		760
d.	Cash	1,200	
	Salaries Expense		1,200

e. The bookkeeper would not make a reversing entry for this transaction.

_____ 2. On December 31, 19X1, X Company accrued salaries expense with an adjusting entry. No reversing entry was made and the payment of the salaries during January 19X2 was correctly recorded. If X Company had recorded an entry on January 1, 19X2, to reverse the accrual, and the subsequent payment was correctly recorded, the effect on the 19X2 financial statements of using the reversing entry would have been:

a. to increase net income and reduce liabilities.
b. to increase 19X2 expense and reduce assets.
c. to decrease 19X2 expense and increase liabilities.
d. to decrease 19X2 expense and decrease liabilities.
e. No effect.

Problem VIII (This problem applies to Appendix B.)

Based on the following end-of-period information, prepare reversing entries assuming that adjusting and closing entries have been properly recorded.

1) Depreciation on office equipment, $3,000.
2) $350 of the $1,400 Prepaid Insurance balance has expired.
3) Employees have earned salaries of $1,000 that have not been paid. They will be paid $1,750 on the next pay date.
4) The company has earned $3,050 of service fees that have not been collected or recorded.
5) The Unearned Service Fees account balance includes $1,000 that has been earned.
6) An inventory of supplies shows $250 of unused supplies. The balance of supplies on the unadjusted trial balance for the period is $900.
7) The company pays $1,200 interest on a loan each quarter. The next quarterly payment is due in two months from the end of the current period.

GENERAL JOURNAL
Page 1

DATE	ACCOUNT TITLES AND EXPLANATION	P.R.	DEBIT	CREDIT

Solutions for Chapter 4

Problem I

1. T
2. F
3. T
4. F
5. F

Problem II

1. B
2. D
3. A
4. B
5. E
6. C

Problem III

Problem IV

1. the adjustments are entered in the accounts
2. debited, credited
3. (a) Is the item a debit or a credit?
   (b) On which statement does it appear?
4. credited, debited
5. Unadjusted Trial Balance columns; adjustments; adjusted trial balance
6. zero
7. zero, zero
8. temporary or nominal, revenue, expense
9. revenue

Problem V

HOMER'S HOME SHOP
Work Sheet for Year Ended December 31, 19—

	Unadjusted Trial Balance		Adjustments		Adjusted Trial Balance		Income Statement		Statement of Ch. in O.E. and Balance Sheet	
	Dr.	Cr.	Dr.	Cr.	Dr.	Cr.	Dr.	Cr.	Dr.	Cr.
Cash	2,875				2,875				2,875	
Accounts receivable	2,000				2,000				2,000	
Shop supplies	1,762			(a) 1,037	725				725	
Shop equipment	5,125				5,125				5,125	
Accum. depr., shop equipment		725		(b) 475		1,200				1,200
Accounts payable		575				575				575
Homer Tonely, capital		5,500				5,500				5,500
Homer Tonely, withdrawals	30,000				30,000				30,000	
Repair services revenue		55,785				55,785		55,785		
Wages expense	18,250		(c) 388		18,638		18,638			
Rent expense	2,500				2,500		2,500			
Miscellaneous expenses	73				73		73			
	62,585	62,585								
Shop supplies expense			(a) 1,037		1,037		1,037			
Depreciation expense, shop equipment			(b) 475		475		475			
Wages payable				(c) 388		388				388
			1,900	1,900	63,448	63,448	22,723	55,785	40,725	7,663
Net income							33,062			33,062
							55,785	55,785	40,725	40,725

Dec. 31 Shop Supplies Expense 1,037
         Shop Supplies 1,037

31 Depr. Expense, Shop Equipment 475
      Accumulated Depr., Shop Equipment 475

31 Wages Expense 388
      Wages Payable 388

31 Repair Services Revenue 55,785
      Income Summary 55,785

31 Income Summary 22,723
      Rent Expense 2,500
      Wages Expense 18,638
      Miscellaneous Expenses 73
      Shop Supplies Expense 1,037
      Depr. Expense, Shop Equipment 475

31 Income Summary 33,062
      Homer Tonely, Capital 33,062

31 Homer Tonely, Capital 30,000
      Homer Tonely, Withdrawals 30,000

GENERAL LEDGER

Cash

Date	Debit	Credit	Balance
Dec. 31			2,875.00

Accounts Receivable

Date	Debit	Credit	Balance
Dec. 31			2,000.00

Shop Supplies

Date	Debit	Credit	Balance
Dec. 31			1,762.00
31		1,037.00	725.00

Shop Equipment

Date	Debit	Credit	Balance
Dec. 31			5,125.00

Accum. Depr., Shop Equipment

Date	Debit	Credit	Balance
Dec. 31			725.00
31		475.00	1,200.00

Accounts Payable

Date	Debit	Credit	Balance
Dec. 31			575.00

Wages Payable

Date	Debit	Credit	Balance
Dec. 31		388.00	388.00

Homer Tonely, Capital

Date	Debit	Credit	Balance
Dec. 31			5,500.00
31		33,062.00	38,562.00
31	30,000.00		8,562.00

Homer Tonely, Withdrawals

Date	Debit	Credit	Balance
Dec. 31			30,000.00
31		30,000.00	-0-

Repair Services Revenue

Date	Debit	Credit	Balance
Dec. 31			55,785.00
31	55,785.00		-0-

Depr. Expense, Shop Equipment

Date	Debit	Credit	Balance
Dec. 31	475.00		475.00
31		475.00	-0-

Wages Expense

Date	Debit	Credit	Balance
Dec. 31			18,250.00
31	388.00		18,638.00
31		18,638.00	-0-

Rent Expense

Date	Debit	Credit	Balance
Dec. 31			2,500.00
31		2,500.00	-0-

Shop Supplies Expense

Date	Debit	Credit	Balance
Dec. 31	1,037.00		1,037.00
31		1,037.00	-0-

Miscellaneous Expenses

Date	Debit	Credit	Balance
Dec. 31			73.00
31		73.00	-0-

Income Summary

Date	Debit	Credit	Balance
Dec. 31		55,785.00	55,785.00
31	22,723.00		33,062.00
31	33,062.00		-0-

HOMER'S HOME SHOP
Post-Closing Trial Balance
December 31, 19—

Cash	$ 2,875	
Accounts receivable	2,000	
Shop supplies	725	
Shop equipment	5,125	
Accumulated depreciation, shop equipment		$ 1,200
Accounts payable		575
Wages payable		388
Homer Tonely, capital		8,562
	$10,725	$10,725

Problem VI

1. T
2. F
3. T

Problem VII

1. C
2. E

Problem VIII

1) No reversing entry required.

2) No reversing entry required.

3) Salaries Payable 1,000.00
       Salaries Expense 1,000.00

4) Service Fees Earned 3,050.00
       Accounts Receivable 3,050.00

5) No reversing entry required.

6) No reversing entry required.

7) Interest Payable 400.00
       Interest Expense 400.00

5 Accounting for Merchandising Activities

Learning Objective 1:

Describe merchandising activities, analyze their effects on financial statements, and record sales of merchandise.

Summary

Merchandising companies purchase and sell products. Their financial statements include the cost of the merchandise inventory in the current assets on the balance sheet and sales and cost of goods sold on the income statement. The difference between the sales and cost of goods sold is called the gross profit.

The seller of merchandise records the sale at the list price less any trade discount. Any returns or allowances are recorded in a contra account to provide information to the manager. When cash discounts from the sales price are offered and the customers pay within the discount period, the seller records the discounts in a contra sales account.

Learning Objective 2:

Describe how the ending inventory and the cost of goods sold are determined with perpetual and periodic inventory accounting systems.

Summary

A perpetual inventory system continuously tracks the cost of goods on hand and the cost of goods sold. A periodic system merely accumulates the cost of goods purchased during the year and does not provide continuous information about the cost of the inventory or the sold goods. At year-end, the cost of the inventory is determined and used to calculate the cost of goods sold. The cost of goods available for sale equals the beginning inventory plus the cost of goods purchased. The cost of goods sold equals the cost of goods available for sale minus the cost of the ending inventory. The cost of goods purchased is affected by purchases discounts, purchases returns and allowances, and transportation-in. These amounts are recorded in contra and supplemental accounts to provide information to management. The contra and supplemental accounts are seldom reported in external statements.

Learning Objective 3:

Describe various formats for income statements and prepare closing entries for a merchandising business.

Summary

Companies have flexibility in choosing formats for their income statements. Internal statements have more details, including the calculations of net sales and the cost of goods sold. Classified income statements describe expenses incurred in different activities. Multiple-step statements include several intermediate totals and single-step statements do not. In the closing entry approach, the Merchandise Inventory account is updated in the process of making closing entries. The ending inventory amount is added to the account as part of the entry that closes the income statement accounts with credit balances. The beginning inventory amount is removed from the account as part of the entry that closes the income statement accounts with debit balances.

Learning Objective 4:

Complete a work sheet for a merchandising company and explain the difference between the closing entry and adjusting entry approaches to updating the Merchandise Inventory account.

Summary

The work sheet for a merchandising company uses special entries to update the inventory. The beginning inventory balance is extended into the Income Statement Debit column and the cost of the ending inventory is entered in the Income Statement Credit column and Balance Sheet Debit column. Many accountants omit the adjusted trial balance columns to reduce the size of the work sheet. The adjusting entry approach to recording the ending inventory in the accounts uses two adjusting entries that remove the beginning cost from and add the ending cost to the Merchandise Inventory account. This approach is often used in computer systems.

Learning Objective 5:

Calculate the acid-test ratio and describe what it reveals about a company's liquidity.

Summary

The acid-test ratio is used to assess a company's ability to pay its current liabilities with its existing quick assets (cash, short-term investments, and receivables). The costs of the merchandise inventory and prepaid expenses are not included in the numerator. A ratio value equal to or greater than one is usually considered to be adequate.

Learning Objective 6:

Define or explain the words and phrases listed in the chapter glossary.

Summary

See Problem III.

Topical Outline

I. Accounting for a merchandising company differs from accounting for a service enterprise.

    A. Net income of a service company is fees, fares, or commissions earned less operating expenses.

    B. Net income of a merchandising company is sales revenue less cost of goods sold and operating expenses.

    C. Net sales less cost of goods sold equals gross profit—the "profit" before operating expenses are deducted.

II. Net sales is:

    A. Sales—total cash and credit sales before any deductions—;

    B. Less sales returns and allowances—the sales value of merchandise returned by customers and deductions from the sales price granted to customers for unsatisfactory goods—;

    C. Less sales discounts—deductions from the invoice price granted to customers in return for early payment.

III. Inventory accounting systems

    A. Perpetual inventory system—maintains continuous records of the amount of inventory on hand and sold.

    B. Periodic inventory system—records the cost of inventory purchased but does not continuously update the records of the quantity and cost of goods on hand or sold. The records are periodically updated to reflect the physical inventory of merchandise on hand.

IV. Cost of goods sold and the periodic inventory system

    A. Merchandise inventory at the end of one period is the beginning inventory of the next period.

    B. Cost of merchandise purchased includes the gross purchase price less purchases (cash) discounts and purchases returns and allowances, plus transportation-in.

        1. FOB shipping point—buyer pays shipping costs.

        2. FOB destination—seller pays shipping costs.

    C. Cost of goods sold is calculated as the cost of beginning inventory plus the cost of merchandise purchased less the cost of ending inventory.

    D. Inventory shrinkage is automatically included in the cost of goods sold.

V. Trade discounts

    A. Deductions from list price to arrive at invoice price.

    B. Not separately entered in the accounts of seller or purchaser. Transaction is recorded using invoice price.

VI. Debit and credit memoranda

    A. Debit memorandum—informs the recipient that the sender has debited the account receivable or payable.

    B. Credit memorandum—informs the recipient that the sender has credited the account receivable or payable.

VII. Income statement alternatives for a merchandising company

    A. Classified income statement

    B. Multiple-step income statement

    C. Single-step income statement

VIII. Closing entries

    A. Record ending inventory and close temporary accounts with credit balances.

    B. Remove beginning inventory and close temporary accounts with debit balances.

    C. Close the Income Summary account to the owner's capital account.

    D. Close the withdrawals account to the owner's capital account.

IX. Preparing a work sheet for a merchandising company—follow the same procedures as explained in Chapter 4 for a service company. (Note, however, that the work sheet presented in Chapter 5 does not include adjusted trial balance columns.)

    A. Extend the beginning inventory balance to the Income Statement Debit column.

    B. Enter the ending inventory balance in the Income Statement Credit column and in the Statement of Changes in Owner's Equity and Balance Sheet Debit column.

X. Adjusting entry approach

    A. Prepare the following adjusting entries:

        1. Debit Income Summary and credit Merchandise Inventory for beginning inventory.

        2. Debit Merchandise Inventory and credit Income Summary for ending inventory.

    B. Prepare closing entries to close the temporary accounts. (These do not include the Merchandise Inventory account.)

    C. The Income Summary account is included on the bottom of the work sheet and the Merchandise Inventory adjusting entries are recorded in the Adjustments columns.

XI. Acid-test ratio

    A. Used to assess the company's ability to settle its current debts with its existing assets.

    B. Calculated as: $\dfrac{\text{Quick assets}}{\text{Current liabilities}}$

Problem I

The following statements are either true or false. Place a (T) in the parentheses before each true statement and an (F) before each false statement.

1. ( ) Sales returns and allowances or discounts are not included in the calculation of net sales.

2. ( ) Ending inventory is subtracted from the cost of goods available for sale to determine cost of goods sold.

3. ( ) In a periodic inventory system, a physical count is taken of the merchandise on hand to determine the correct amount of inventory.

4. ( ) When a periodic inventory system is used, inventory losses are absorbed in cost of goods sold.

5. ( ) Quick assets include cash, short-term investments, receivables and merchandise inventory.

6. ( ) Under the adjusting entry approach to recording the change in the Merchandise Inventory account, the closing entries do not reflect changes in the Merchandise Inventory account.

7. ( ) Both the adjusting entry and closing entry approaches to recording the change in the Merchandise Inventory account result in the same balances in the Income Summary account.

8. ( ) Under the closing entry approach to recording the change in the Merchandise Inventory account, the closing entry in which the Income Summary account is credited to close revenue and cost of goods sold accounts that have credit balances also enters the ending inventory amount in the Merchandise Inventory account.

9. ( ) A debit or credit memorandum may originate with either party to a transaction, but the memorandum gets its name from the action of the selling party exclusively.

Problem II

You are given several words, phrases, or numbers to choose from in completing each of the following statements or in answering the following questions. In each case select the one that best completes the statement or answers the question and place its letter in the answer space provided.

_____ 1. A method of accounting for inventories in which cost of goods sold is recorded each time a sale is made and an up-to-date record of goods on hand is maintained is called a:

a. product inventory system.
b. perpetual inventory system.
c. periodic inventory system.
d. parallel inventory system.
e. principal inventory system.

_____ 2. Based on the following information, calculate the missing amounts.

Sales	$28,800	Cost of goods sold	?
Beginning inventory	?	Gross profit	$10,800
Purchases	18,000	Expenses	?
Ending inventory	12,600	Net income	3,600

a. Beginning inventory, $16,200; Cost of goods sold, $12,600; Expenses, $1,800.
b. Beginning inventory, $23,400; Cost of goods sold, $10,800; Expenses, $7,200.
c. Beginning inventory, $9,000; Cost of goods sold, $14,400; Expenses, $3,600.
d. Beginning inventory, $12,600; Cost of goods sold, $18,000; Expenses, $7,200.
e. Beginning inventory, $19,800; Cost of goods sold, $25,200; Expenses, $14,400.

3. What is the effect on the income statement at the end of an accounting period in which the ending inventory of the prior period was understated and carried forward incorrectly?

   a. Cost of goods sold is overstated and net income is understated.
   b. Cost of goods sold is understated and net income is understated.
   c. Cost of goods sold is understated and net income is overstated.
   d. Cost of goods sold is overstated and net income is overstated.
   e. The errors of the prior period and the current period offset each other, so there is no effect on the income statement.

4. The following information is taken from a single proprietorship's income statement. Calculate ending inventory for the business.

Sales	$165,250	Purchases returns	$	390
Sales returns	980	Purchases discounts		1,630
Sales discounts	1,960	Transportation-in		700
Beginning inventory	16,880	Gross profit		58,210
Purchases	108,380	Net income		17,360

   a. $19,840.
   b. $22,080.
   c. $21,160.
   d. $44,250.
   e. Some other amount.

5. On July 18, Double Aught Sales Company sold merchandise on credit, terms 2/10, n/30, $1,080. On July 21, Double Aught issued a $180 credit memorandum to the customer of July 18 who returned a portion of the merchandise purchased. What is Double Aught's journal entry to record the July 21 transaction?

   a. Accounts Receivable 180.00
        Sales 180.00
   b. Sales Returns and Allowances 180.00
        Accounts Receivable 180.00
   c. Accounts Receivable 900.00
        Sales Returns and Allowances 180.00
        Sales 1,080.00
   d. Sales 180.00
        Accounts Receivable 180.00
   e. Sales Returns and Allowances 180.00
        Sales 180.00

6. The following information is available from the balance sheet of Foster Company:

Cash	$22,300
Short-term investments	10,500
Accounts receivable	47,360
Merchandise inventory	52,100
Accounts payable	66,800
J. Foster, capital	57,300

Foster's acid-test ratio is:

   a. 0.5
   b. 1.2
   c. 2.0
   d. 1.4
   e. 2.3

Problem III

Many of the important ideas and concepts discussed in Chapter 5 are reflected in the following list of key terms. Test your understanding of these terms by matching the appropriate definitions with the terms. Record the number identifying the most appropriate definition in the blank space next to each term.

_____ Acid-test ratio

_____ Cash discount

_____ Classified income statement

_____ Credit memorandum

_____ Credit period

_____ Credit terms

_____ Debit memorandum

_____ Discount period

_____ EOM

_____ FOB

_____ General and administrative expenses

_____ Gross profit

_____ List price

_____ Merchandise

_____ Merchandise inventory

_____ Multiple-step income statement

_____ Periodic inventory system

_____ Perpetual inventory system

_____ Purchases discount

_____ Sales discount

_____ Selling expenses

_____ Shrinkage

_____ Single-step income statement

_____ Trade discount

1. The difference between net sales and the cost of goods sold.

2. A method of accounting that maintains continuous records of the amount of inventory on hand and sold.

3. A reduction below a list or catalog price that is negotiated in setting the selling price of goods.

4. A cash discount taken by customers against an amount owed to the seller.

5. A notification that the sender has entered a debit in the recipient's account maintained by the sender.

6. An income statement format that shows several intermediate totals between sales and net income.

7. The abbreviation for *end-of-month;* used to describe credit terms for some transactions.

8. The nominal price of an item before any trade discount is deducted.

9. Goods a company owns on any given date and holds for the purpose of selling them to its customers.

10. The description of the amounts and timing of payments that a buyer agrees to make in the future.

11. The time period that can pass before a customer's payment is due.

12. A ratio used to assess the company's ability to settle its current debts with its existing assets; it is the ratio between a company's quick assets (cash, short-term investments, and receivables) and its current liabilities.

13. A cash discount taken against an amount owed to a supplier of goods.

14. A notification that the sender has entered a credit in the recipient's account maintained by the sender.

15. A method of accounting that records the cost of inventory purchased but does not track the quantity on hand or sold to customers; the records are updated periodically to reflect the results of physical counts of the items on hand.

16. The time period in which a cash discount is available.

17. An income statement format that does not present intermediate totals other than total expenses.

18. A reduction in a debt that is granted by a seller to a purchaser in exchange for the purchaser's making payment within a specified period of time called the discount period.

19. The expenses of promoting sales by displaying and advertising the merchandise, making sales, and delivering goods to customers.

20. Goods acquired for the purpose of reselling them to customers.

21. Expenses that support the overall operations of a business and include the expenses of such activities as providing accounting services, human resource management, and financial management.

22. The abbreviation for *free on board;* the designated point at which ownership of goods passes to the buyer.

23. An income statement format that classifies items in significant groups and shows detailed calculations of sales and cost of goods sold.

24. Inventory losses that occur as a result of shoplifting or deterioration.

Problem IV

Below is the Valentine Variety Store work sheet for the year ended December 31, 19X2. Note that the format of this work sheet includes the Adjusted Trial Balance columns as presented in Chapter 4. Sort the adjusted trial balance amounts into the proper financial statement columns and finish the work sheet. The December 31, 19X2, inventory is $15,000.

VALENTINE VARIETY STORE
Work Sheet, December 31, 19X2

ACCOUNT	ADJUSTED TRIAL BALANCE		INCOME STATEMENT		STATEMENT OF CHANGES IN O.E. AND BALANCE SHEET	
	DR.	CR.	DR.	CR.	DR.	CR.
Cash	40000 00					
Merchandise inventory	130000 00					
Other assets	80000 00					
Liabilities		40000 00				
Violet Valentine, capital		223000 00				
Violet Valentine, withdrawals	100000 00					
Sales		800000 00				
Sales returns and allowances	60000 00					
Purchases	485000 00					
Purchases returns and allowances		40000 00				
Purchases discounts		90000 00				
Transportation-in	250000 00					
General and admin. expenses	80000 00					
Selling expenses	130000 00					
	1076000 00	1076000 00				
Net income						

Problem V

After finishing the work sheet, use the information in its Income Statement columns to complete the following income statement.

VALENTINE VARIETY STORE

Income Statement

For the Year Ended December 31, 19X2

Revenue:					
Sales					
Less: Sales returns and allowances					
Net sales					
Cost of goods sold:					
Merchandise inventory, December 31, 19X1					
Purchases					
Less: Purchases returns					
and allowances $ _____					
Purchases discounts _____					
Net purchases					
Add: Transportation-in					
Cost of goods purchased					
Goods available for sale					
Merchandise inventory, December 31, 19X2					
Cost of goods sold					
Gross profit from sales					
Operating expenses:					
General and administrative expenses					
Selling expenses					
Total operating expenses					
Net income					

Problem VI

Prepare the closing entries for Valentine Variety Store. Do not give explanations, but skip a line after each entry.

GENERAL JOURNAL   Page 1

DATE	ACCOUNT TITLES AND EXPLANATION	P.R.	DEBIT	CREDIT

Problem VII

Below is the Merchandise Inventory account of Valentine Variety Store as it appeared before the 19X2 closing entries were posted. Note that its $13,000 debit balance shows the amount of the December 31, 19X1, inventory which was posted to the account when the closing entries were made at the end of 19X1. From the closing entries that were journalized in Part VI, post the appropriate amounts to the Merchandise Inventory account below.

GENERAL LEDGER

Merchandise Inventory   Account No. 119

DATE	EXPLANATION	P.R.	DEBIT	CREDIT	BALANCE
19X1 Dec. 31		G-3	13 000 00		13 000 00

Problem VIII

1. If a company determines cost of goods sold by counting the inventory at the end of the period and subtracting the inventory from the cost of goods available for sale, the system of accounting for inventories is called a(n) _____ .

2. Trade discounts _____ (are, are not) credited to the Purchases Discounts account.

3. A reduction in a payable that is granted if it is paid within the discount period is a _____ discount.

4. A store received a credit memorandum from a wholesaler for unsatisfactory merchandise the store had returned for credit. The store should record the memorandum with a _____ (debit, credit) to its Purchases Returns and Allowances account and a _____ (debit, credit) to its Accounts Payable account.

5. The two common systems of accounting for merchandise inventories are the _____ inventory system and the _____ inventory system. Before the availability of computers, the _____ inventory system was most likely used in stores that sold a large volume of relatively low-priced items.

Problem IX

The trial balance that follows was taken from the ledger of Sporthaus Lindner at the end of its annual accounting period. Fritz Lindner, the owner of Sporthaus Lindner, did not make additional investments in the business during 19X1.

SPORTHAUS LINDNER
Unadjusted Trial Balance
December 31, 19X1

Cash	$ 1,840	
Accounts receivable	2,530	
Merchandise inventory	3,680	
Store supplies	2,070	
Accounts payable		$ 4,370
Salaries payable	---	---
Fritz Lindner, capital		5,980
Fritz Lindner, withdrawals	1,380	
Sales		14,260
Sales returns and allowances	1,150	
Purchases	5,750	
Purchases discounts		920
Transportation-in	1,150	
Salaries expense	4,370	
Rent expense	1,610	
Store supplies expense	---	---
Totals	$25,530	$25,530

Use the adjusting entry approach to account for merchandise inventories and prepare adjusting journal entries and closing journal entries for Sporthaus Lindner using the following information:

a. Ending store supplies inventory, $1,150.
b. Accrued salaries payable, $690.
c. Ending merchandise inventory, $4,830.

DATE	ACCOUNT TITLES AND EXPLANATION	P.R.	DEBIT	CREDIT

Solutions for Chapter 5

Problem I

1.	F	6.	T
2.	T	7.	T
3.	T	8.	T
4.	T	9.	F
5.	F		

Problem II

1.	B
2.	D
3.	C
4.	A
5.	B
6.	B

Problem III

Acid-test ratio	12	List price	8
Cash discount	18	Merchandise	20
Classified income statement	23	Merchandise inventory	9
Credit memorandum	14	Multiple-step income statement	6
Credit period	11	Periodic inventory system	15
Credit terms	10	Perpetual inventory system	2
Debit memorandum	5	Purchases discount	13
Discount period	16	Sales discount	4
EOM	7	Selling expenses	19
FOB	22	Shrinkage	24
General and administrative expenses	21	Single-step income statement	17
Gross profit	1	Trade discount	3

Problem IV

VALENTINE VARIETY STORE
Work Sheet, December 31, 19X2

	Adjusted Trial Balance		Income Statement		St. of Ch. in O.E. and Balance Sh.	
	Dr.	Cr.	Dr.	Cr.	Dr.	Cr.
Cash	4,000	....	......	......	4,000	......
Merchandise inventory	13,000	....	13,000	15,000	15,000	......
Other assets	8,000	....	......	......	8,000	......
Liabilities	....	4,000	......	......	......	4,000
Violet Valentine, capital	....	22,300	......	......	......	22,300
Violet Valentine, withdrawals	10,000	....	......	......	10,000	......
Sales	....	80,000	......	80,000	......	......
Sales returns and allowances	600	....	600	......	......	......
Purchases	48,500	....	48,500	......	......	......
Purchases returns and allowances	....	400	......	400	......	......
Purchases discounts	....	900	......	900	......	......
Transportation-in	2,500	....	2,500	......	......	......
General and administrative expenses	8,000	....	8,000	......	......	......
Selling expenses	13,000	....	13,000	....	....	....
	107,600	107,600	85,600	96,300	37,000	26,300
Net income			10,700	......	......	10,700
			96,300	96,300	37,000	37,000

Problem V

VALENTINE VARIETY STORE
Income Statement
For the Year Ended December 31, 19X2

Revenue:			
Sales		$80,000	
Less: Sales returns and allowances		600	
Net sales			$79,400
Cost of goods sold:			
Merchandise inventory, December 31, 19X1		$13,000	
Purchases	$48,500		
Less: Purchases returns and allowances	$400		
Purchases discounts	900	1,300	
Net purchases		$47,200	
Add: Transportation-in		2,500	
Cost of goods purchased		49,700	
Goods available for sale		$62,700	
Merchandise inventory, December 31, 19X2		15,000	
Cost of goods sold			47,700
Gross profit from sales			$31,700
Operating expenses:			
General and administrative expenses		$ 8,000	
Selling expenses		13,000	
Total operating expenses			21,000
Net income			$10,700

Problem VI

Dec. 31	Income Summary	85,600.00	
	Merchandise Inventory		13,000.00
	Sales Returns and Allowances		600.00
	Purchases		48,500.00
	Transportation-In		2,500.00
	General and Administrative Expenses		8,000.00
	Selling Expenses		13,000.00
31	Merchandise Inventory	15,000.00	
	Sales	80,000.00	
	Purchases Returns and Allowances	400.00	
	Purchases Discounts	900.00	
	Income Summary		96,300.00
31	Income Summary	10,700.00	
	Violet Valentine, Capital		10,700.00
31	Violet Valentine, Capital	10,000.00	
	Violet Valentine, Withdrawals		10,000.00

Problem VII

DATE	EXPLANATION	P.R.	DEBIT	CREDIT	BALANCE
19X1 Dec. 31		G-3	13 000 00		13 000 00
19X2					
Dec. 31	.	G-8		13 000 00	- 0 -
31		G-9	15 000 00		15 000 00

Merchandise Inventory — Account No. 119

Problem VIII

1. periodic inventory system
2. are not
3. cash
4. credit, debit
5. periodic, perpetual, periodic

Problem IX

Adjusting Entries

Dec. 31	Store Supplies Expense	920.00	
	Store Supplies		920.00
31	Salaries Expense	690.00	
	Salaries Payable		690.00
31	Income Summary	3,680.00	
	Merchandise Inventory		3,680.00
31	Merchandise Inventory	4,830.00	
	Income Summary		4,830.00

Closing Entries

Dec. 31	Sales	14,260.00	
	Purchases Discounts	920.00	
	Income Summary		15,180.00
31	Income Summary	15,640.00	
	Sales Returns and Allowances		1,150.00
	Purchases		5,750.00
	Transportation-In		1,150.00
	Salaries Expense		5,060.00
	Rent Expense		1,610.00
	Store Supplies Expense		920.00
31	Income Summary	690.00	
	Fritz Lindner, Capital		690.00
31	Fritz Lindner, Capital	1,380.00	
	Fritz Lindner, Withdrawals		1,380.00

6 Accounting Systems

Learning Objective 1:

Describe the five basic components of an accounting system.

Summary

The components of accounting systems include: source documents, input devices, the data processor, data storage, and output devices. Both manual and computerized systems must have all five components.

Learning Objective 2:

Describe the types of computers used in large and small accounting systems, the role of software in those systems, and the different approaches to inputting and processing data, including the use of networking.

Summary

Depending on the complexity of a company's accounting system, the computers used may be large mainframe computers or smaller microcomputers. If a mainframe computer is used, the software that provides the computer instructions is likely to be custom made for the company. However, an increasing variety of off-the-shelf programs are available, especially for microcomputers. There are many different ways to set up computer systems, including batch and on-line processing, and computer networks.

Learning Objective 3:

Explain special journals and controlling accounts, use them to record transactions, and explain how to test the posting of entries to the Accounts Receivable and Accounts Payable subsidiary ledgers.

Summary

Columnar journals are designed so that repetitive debits or credits are entered in separate columns. A typical set of special journals includes a Sales Journal, a Purchases Journal, a Cash Receipts Journal, and a Cash Disbursements Journal (or Check Register). Any transactions that cannot be entered in the special journals are entered in the General Journal.

When many accounts of the same type are required, such as an account receivable for each credit customer, they usually are kept in a separate subsidiary ledger. Then, a single controlling account is maintained in the General Ledger. After all transactions are posted to the accounts in the subsidiary ledger and to the controlling account, the controlling account balance should equal the sum of the account balances in the subsidiary ledger.

Learning Objective 4:

Explain the use of special and general journals in accounting for sales taxes and sales returns and allowances, and explain how sales invoices can serve as a Sales Journal.

Summary

To record sales taxes, the Sales Journal and the Cash Receipts Journal should include a separate Sales Taxes Payable column. When sales invoices substitute for a Sales Journal, the customer accounts in the Accounts Receivable Ledger are posted directly from the sales invoices. Copies of the invoices for each month are then bound and totaled as a basis for recording the sales in the General Ledger. Sales returns and allowances may be recorded in the General Journal, or a special journal for sales returns and allowances may be used.

Learning Objective 5:

Explain the nature and use of business segment information.

Summary

Public companies with material operations in more than one industry must provide separate information for each segment. The information includes revenues, operating profits, capital expenditures, depreciation, and identifiable assets. It also includes a geographical distribution of sales and sales to major customers.

Learning Objective 6:

Define or explain the words and phrases listed in the chapter glossary.

Summary

See Problem III.

Topical Outline

I. Accounting systems

   A. Consist of people, forms, procedures, and equipment.

   B. Generally include the basic components of: source documents, input devices, data processor, data storage, and output devices.

II. Computer-based systems

   A. May use both personal computers (or microcomputers) which are small, inexpensive, and easy to operate, and mainframes, which are large and capable of quickly processing huge quantities of data.

   B. Software programs can be custom designed or off-the-shelf (ready to use).

   C. Input may be entered using batch processing or on-line processing.

   D. Computer networks allow users to share access to the same data and the same programs.

III. Subsidiary ledgers

   A. Information about the amounts purchased, the amounts paid, and the amounts owed by each customer requires a separate accounts receivable account for each customer. These accounts are usually maintained in a subsidiary ledger called an Accounts Receivable Ledger. Separate accounts for creditors are maintained in an Accounts Payable Ledger.

   B. Each subsidiary ledger is represented by a controlling account in the General Ledger.

   C. The accuracy of a subsidiary ledger is periodically tested by preparing a schedule of accounts receivable (or payable, etc.). The sum of the accounts in the ledger should equal the controlling account's balance.

IV. Special journals

   A. Reduce writing and posting labor, by grouping similar transactions together and recording them in one place and periodically posting totals accumulated.

   B. Examples:

      1. Sales Journal—typically a single column journal in which all credit sales but no other transactions are recorded.

         a. Individual entries in the Sales Journal are posted to the accounts in the subsidiary Accounts Receivable Ledger.

         b. The column total of the Sales Journal is posted as a debit to Accounts Receivable and as a credit to Sales in the General Ledger.

      2. Cash Receipts Journal—a multicolumn journal in which all cash receipts but no other transactions are recorded.

         a. A column titled "Other Accounts - Credit" is used to record all types of receipts that are not frequent enough to justify having separate columns. Each credit in the Other Accounts column must be posted individually.

         b. Separate credit columns, for which only the totals are posted, are usually established for Accounts Receivable and Sales. A separate debit column may be used for sales discounts.

3. Purchases Journal—all credit purchases but no cash purchases are recorded in this journal. Also, separate columns may be established for frequent credit purchases such as store supplies and office supplies.

   a. Credits to the accounts of particular creditors are individually posted to the subsidiary Accounts Payable Ledger.

4. Cash Disbursements Journal—all cash payments except those made from petty cash are recorded in this journal. (A reimbursement of petty cash is, however, recorded in the Cash Disbursements Journal.)

   a. A Check Register is a cash disbursements journal that includes a column for entering the number of each check.

   b. An "Other Accounts - Debit" column is necessary so that the journal can accommodate all types of cash payments.

5. General Journal—must be provided even when special journals are used.

   a. Allows the recording of entries which do not fit under any of the special journals.

   b. Examples are:
      1. Adjusting entries.
      2. Closing entries.
      3. Correcting entries.
      4. Other transactions may include sales returns, purchases returns, and purchases of plant assets.

C. Alternative uses of special journals

   1. If a company collects sales taxes from its customers, the Sales Journal usually has a separate column in which the taxes are recorded.

   2. In some companies, a collection of all sales invoices serves as a Sales Journal.

   3. Sales returns may be recorded in the General Journal, or a separate Sales Returns and Allowances Journal is sometimes used.

V. Business segment information

A. Business segment—a portion of a company that can be separately identified by the products or services it provides or a geographic market it serves.

B. Public companies with material operations in more than one industry are required to publilsh separate information for each segment, including:

   1. Revenues or net sales.
   2. Operating profits (before interest and taxes).
   3. Capital expenditures.
   4. Depreciation and amortization expense.
   5. Identifiable assets.
   6. In some cases, a geographical distribution of sales.
   7. In some cases, sales to major customers that account for 10% or more of total sales.

Problem I

The following statements are either true or false. Place a (T) in the parentheses before each true statement and an (F) before each false statement.

1. ( ) A Purchases Journal is used to record all purchases.

2. ( ) At month-end, the total sales recorded in the Sales Journal is debited to Accounts Receivable and credited to Sales.

3. ( ) Sales is a General Ledger account.

4. ( ) Transactions recorded in a journal do not necessarily result in equal debits and credits to General Ledger accounts.

5. ( ) If a general journal entry is used to record a charge sale, the credit of the entry must be posted twice.

6. ( ) A printer is one example of an input device for a computer system.

7. ( ) Business segment information is required of all U.S. companies.

Problem II

You are given several words, phrases or numbers to choose from in completing each of the following statements or in answering the following questions. In each case select the one that best completes the statement or answers the question and place its letter in the answer space provided.

_____ 1. A company that uses a Sales Journal, a Purchases Journal, a Cash Receipts Journal, a Cash Disbursements Journal, and a General Journal borrowed $1,500 from the bank in exchange for a note payable to the bank. In which journal would the transaction be recorded?

    a. Sales Journal.
    b. Purchases Journal.
    c. Cash Receipts Journal.
    d. Cash Disbursements Journal.
    e. General Journal.

_____ 2. A company that uses a Sales Journal, a Purchases Journal, a Cash Receipts Journal, a Cash Disbursements Journal, and a General Journal paid a creditor for office supplies purchased on account. In which journal would the transaction be recorded?

    a. Sales Journal.
    b. Purchases Journal.
    c. Cash Receipts Journal.
    d. Cash Disbursements Journal.
    e. General Journal.

_____ 3. A book of original entry that is designed and used for recording only a specified type of transaction is a:

    a. Check Register.
    b. subsidiary ledger.
    c. General Ledger.
    d. special journal.
    e. Schedule of Accounts Payable.

_____ 4. A company that accumulates source documents for a period of time and then processes all at the same time:

    a. is most likely an airline company.
    b. must be using a manual accounting system.
    c. uses batch processing.
    d. uses on-line processing.
    e. always has an up-to-date data base.

Problem III

Many of the important ideas and concepts discussed in Chapter 6 are reflected in the following list of key terms. Test your understanding of these terms by matching the appropriate definitions with the terms. Record the number identifying the most appropriate definition in the blank space next to each term.

_____ Accounting system   _____ Data storage

_____ Accounts Payable Ledger   _____ General Ledger

_____ Accounts Receivable Ledger   _____ Input device

_____ Batch processing   _____ On-line processing

_____ Business segment   _____ Output devices

_____ Check Register   _____ Schedule of accounts payable

_____ Columnar journal   _____ Schedule of accounts receivable

_____ Computer network   _____ Special journal

_____ Controlling account   _____ Subsidiary ledger

_____ Data processor

1. A means of transferring information from source documents to the data processing component of an accounting system.

2. A book of original entry for recording cash payments by check.

3. The component of an accounting system that keeps the inputted data in a readily accessible manner so that financial reports can be drawn from it efficiently.

4. A list of the balances of all the accounts in the Accounts Receivable Ledger that is summed to show the total amount of accounts receivable outstanding.

5. A general ledger account the balance of which (after posting) equals the sum of the balances of the accounts in a related subsidiary ledger.

6. The people, forms, procedures, and equipment that are used to capture data about the transactions of an entity and to generate from that data a variety of financial, managerial, and tax accounting reports.

7. The ledger that contains the financial statement accounts of a business.

8. A book of original entry that is designed and used for recording only a specified type of transaction.

9. An approach to inputting data that accumulates source documents for a period such as a day, week, or month and inputs all of them at the same time.

10. A subsidiary ledger that contains a separate account for each party that grants credit on account to the entity.

11. A list of the balances of all the accounts in the Accounts Payable Ledger that is summed to show the total amount of accounts payable outstanding.

12. The component of an accounting system that interprets, manipulates, and summarizes the recorded information so that it can be used in analyses and reports.

13. A subsidiary ledger that contains an account for each credit customer.

14. An approach to inputting data whereby the data on each source document is inputted as soon as the document is available.

15. A group of accounts which show the details underlying the balance of a controlling account in the General Ledger.

16. The means by which information is taken out of the accounting system and made available for use.

17. A book of original entry having columns, each of which is designated as the place for entering specific data about each transaction of a group of similar transactions.

18. A system in which computers are linked with each other so that different users on different computers can share access to the same data and the same programs.

19. A portion of a company that can be separately identified by the products or services that it provides or a geographic market that it serves.

Problem IV

Complete the following by filling in the blanks.

1. The five basic components of an accounting system are: source documents, _____, the data processor, _____, and output devices.

2. When a company records sales returns with general journal entries, the credit of an entry recording such a return is posted to two different accounts. This does not cause the trial balance to be out of balance because _____

_____ .

3. Cash sales _____ (are, are not) normally recorded in the Sales Journal.

4. When special journals are used, credit purchases of store supplies or office supplies should be recorded in the _____ .

5. The posting principle upon which a subsidiary ledger and its controlling account operate requires that the controlling account be debited for an amount or amounts equal to the sum of _____ _____ to the subsidiary ledger and that the controlling account be credited for an amount or amounts equal to the sum of _____ to the subsidiary ledger.

6. Cash purchases of store supplies or office supplies should be recorded in a(n) _____ _____ .

7. When a subsidiary Accounts Receivable Ledger is maintained, the equality of the debits and credits posted to the General Ledger is proved by preparing _____ . At the same time the balances of the customer accounts in the Accounts Receivable Ledger are proved by preparing _____ .

8. Business _____ information is required of public companies with material operations in more than one industry. The categories of required reporting information include: revenues, _____ (before interest and taxes), capital expenditures, depreciation and amortization expense, and _____ .

Problem V

Below are eight transactions completed by McGuff Company on September 30 of this year. Following the transactions are the company's journals with prior September transactions recorded therein.

Requirement One: Record the eight transactions in the company's journals.

Sept. 30   Received an $808.50 check from Ted Clark in full payment of the September 20, $825 sale, less the $16.50 discount.

30   Received a $550 check from a tenant in payment of his October rent.

30   Sold merchandise to Inez Smythe on credit, Invoice No. 655, $1,675.

30   Received merchandise and an invoice dated September 28, terms 2/10, n/60 from Johnson Company, $4,000.

30   Purchased store equipment on account from Olson Company, invoice dated September 30, terms n/10, EOM, $950.

30   Issued Check No. 525 to Kerry Meadows in payment of her $650 salary.

30   Issued Check No. 526 for $1,715 to Olson Company in full payment of its September 20 invoice, less a $35 discount.

30   Received a credit memorandum from Olson Company for unsatisfactory merchandise received on September 24 and returned for credit, $625.

30   Cash sales for the last half of the month totaled $9,450.50.

GENERAL JOURNAL
Page 17

DATE	ACCOUNT TITLES AND EXPLANATION	P.R.	DEBIT	CREDIT

SALES JOURNAL
Page 8

DATE	ACCOUNT DEBITED	INVOICE NUMBER	P.R.	AMOUNT
19— Sept. 3	N. R. Boswell	651	√	1,875 00
15	Inez Smythe	652	√	1,500 00
20	Ted Clark	653	√	825 00
24	N. R. Boswell	654	√	2,250 00

DATE	ACCOUNT	DATE OF INVOICE	TERMS	P.R.	PURCHASES DEBIT	OTHER ACCOUNTS DEBIT	ACCOUNTS PAYABLE CREDIT
19— Sept. 8	Johnson Company	9/6	2/10, n/60	√	3 7 5 0 00		3 7 5 0 00
22	Olson Company	9/20	2/10, n/60	√	1 7 5 0 00		1 7 5 0 00
24	Olson Company	9/22	2/10, n/60	√	5 6 2 5 00		5 6 2 5 00

CASH RECEIPTS JOURNAL

DATE	ACCOUNT CREDITED	EXPLANATION	P.R.	OTHER ACCOUNTS CREDIT	ACCOUNTS RECEIVABLE CREDIT	SALES CREDIT	SALES DISCOUNTS DEBIT	CASH DEBIT
19—								
Sept. 1	Rent Earned	Tenant's September rent	406	5 5 0 00				5 5 0 00
13	N. R. Boswell	Full payment of account	√		1 8 7 5 00		3 7 50	1 8 3 7 50
15	Sales	Cash sales	√			9 0 0 0 00		9 0 0 0 00

CASH DISBURSEMENTS JOURNAL

DATE	CH. NO.	PAYEE	ACCOUNT DEBITED	P.R.	OTHER ACCOUNTS DEBIT	ACCOUNTS PAYABLE DEBIT	PURCHASES DISCOUNTS CREDIT	CASH CREDIT
19—								
Sept. 15	523	Kerry Meadows	Salaries Expense	622	6 5 0 00			6 5 0 00
16	524	Johnson Company		√		3 7 5 0 00	7 5 00	3 6 7 5 00

Requirement Two: The individual postings from the journals of McGuff Company through September 29 have been made. Complete the individual postings from the journals.

Requirement Three: Foot and crossfoot the journals and make the month-end postings.

Requirement Four: Complete the trial balance and test the subsidiary ledgers by preparing schedules of accounts receivable and accounts payable.

ACCOUNTS RECEIVABLE LEDGER

N. R. Boswell

2200 Falstaff Street

DATE	EXPLANATION	P.R.	DEBIT	CREDIT	BALANCE
19— Sept. 3		S-8	1 875 00		1 875 00
13		R-9		1 875 00	- 0 -
24		S-8	2 250 00		2 250 00

Ted Clark

10765 Catonsville Avenue

DATE	EXPLANATION	P.R.	DEBIT	CREDIT	BALANCE
19— Sept. 20		S-8	825 00		825 00

Inez Smythe

785 Violette Circle

DATE	EXPLANATION	P.R.	DEBIT	CREDIT	BALANCE
19— Sept. 15		S-8	1 500 00		1 500 00

ACCOUNTS PAYABLE LEDGER

Johnson Company

118 E. Seventh Street

DATE	EXPLANATION	P.R.	DEBIT	CREDIT	BALANCE
19— Sept. 8		P-8		3 750 00	3 750 00
16		D-7	3 750 00		- 0 -

Olson Company

788 Hazelwood Avenue

DATE	EXPLANATION	P.R.	DEBIT	CREDIT	BALANCE
19— Sept. 22		P-8		1 750 00	1 750 00
24		P-8		5 625 00	7 375 00

GENERAL LEDGER

Cash   Account No. 101

DATE	EXPLANATION	P.R.	DEBIT	CREDIT	BALANCE

Accounts Receivable   Account No. 106

DATE	EXPLANATION	P.R.	DEBIT	CREDIT	BALANCE

Store Equipment   Account No. 165

DATE	EXPLANATION	P.R.	DEBIT	CREDIT	BALANCE

Accounts Payable   Account No. 201

DATE	EXPLANATION	P.R.	DEBIT	CREDIT	BALANCE

Rent Earned   Account No. 406

DATE	EXPLANATION	P.R.	DEBIT	CREDIT	BALANCE
19— Sept. 1		R-9		5 5 0 00	5 5 0 00

Sales   Account No. 413

DATE	EXPLANATION	P.R.	DEBIT	CREDIT	BALANCE

Sales Discounts — Account No. 415

DATE	EXPLANATION	P.R.	DEBIT	CREDIT	BALANCE

Purchases — Account No. 505

DATE	EXPLANATION	P.R.	DEBIT	CREDIT	BALANCE

Purchases Discounts — Account No. 507

DATE	EXPLANATION	P.R.	DEBIT	CREDIT	BALANCE

Salaries Expense — Account No. 622

DATE	EXPLANATION	P.R.	DEBIT	CREDIT	BALANCE
19— Sept. 15		D-7	650 00		650 00

MCGUFF COMPANY
Trial Balance
September 30, 19—

Cash			
Accounts receivable			
Store equipment			
Accounts payable			
Rent earned			
Sales			
Sales discounts			
Purchases			
Purchases discounts			
Salaries expense			

MCGUFF COMPANY

Schedule of Accounts Receivable

September 30, 19—

MCGUFF COMPANY

Schedule of Accounts Payable

September 30, 19—

Solutions for Chapter 6

Problem I

1. F
2. T
3. T
4. F
5. F
6. F
7. F

Problem II

1. C
2. B
3. D
4. C

Problem III

Accounting system 6
Accounts Payable Ledger 10
Accounts Receivable Ledger 13
Batch processing 9
Business Segment 19
Check Register 2
Columnar journal 17
Computer network 18
Controlling account 5
Data processor 12

Data storage 3
General Ledger 7
Input device 1
On-line processing 14
Output devices 16
Schedule of accounts payable 11
Schedule of accounts receivable 4
Special journal 8
Subsidiary Ledger 15

Problem IV

1. input devices, data storage

2. only the balance of one of the accounts, the Accounts Receivable account, appears on the trial balance.

3. are not

4. Purchases Journal

5. the debits posted, the credits posted

6. Cash Disbursements Journal

7. a trial balance, a schedule of accounts receivable

8. segment, operating profits, identifiable assets

Problem V

Sept. 30 Accounts Payable—Olson Company .... 201/√ 625.00

          Purchases Returns and Allowances 506   625.00

SALES JOURNAL
Page 8

DATE	ACCOUNT DEBITED	INVOICE NUMBER	P.R.	AMOUNT
19—				
Sept. 3	N. R. Boswell	651	√	1 875 00
15	Inez Smythe	652	√	1 500 00
20	Ted Clark	653	√	825 00
24	N. R. Boswell	654	√	2 250 00
30	Inez Smythe	655	√	1 675 00
30	Accounts Receivable, Dr.; Sales, Cr.			8 125 00
				(106/413)

PURCHASES JOURNAL
Page 8

DATE	ACCOUNT	DATE OF INVOICE	TERMS	P.R.	PURCHASES DEBIT	OTHER ACCOUNTS DEBIT	ACCOUNTS PAYABLE CREDIT
19—							
Sept. 8	Johnson Company	9/6	2/10, n/60	√	3 750 00		3 750 00
22	Olson Company	9/20	2/10, n/60	√	1 750 00		1 750 00
24	Olson Company	9/22	2/10, n/60	√	5 625 00		5 625 00
30	Johnson Company	9/28	2/10, n/60	√	4 000 00		4 000 00
30	Store Equip./Olson Co.	9/30	n/10 EOM	165/√		950 00	950 00
30	Totals				15 125 00	950 00	16 075 00
					(505)	(√)	(201)

CASH RECEIPTS JOURNAL

DATE	ACCOUNT CREDITED	P.R.	OTHER ACCOUNTS CREDIT	ACCOUNTS RECEIVABLE CREDIT	SALES CREDIT	SALES DISCOUNTS DEBIT	CASH DEBIT
19—							
Sept. 1	Rent Earned	406	550 00				550 00
13	N. R. Boswell	✓		1875 00		37 50	1837 50
15	Sales	✓			9000 00		9000 00
30	Ted Clark	✓		825 00		16 50	808 50
30	Rent Earned	406	550 00				550 00
30	Sales	✓			9450 50		9450 50
30	Totals		1100 00	2700 00	18450 50	54 00	22196 50
			(✓)	(106)	(413)	(415)	(101)

CASH DISBURSEMENTS JOURNAL

DATE	CH. NO.	PAYEE	ACCOUNT DEBITED	P.R.	OTHER ACCOUNTS DEBIT	ACCOUNTS PAYABLE DEBIT	PURCHASES DISCOUNT CREDIT	CASH CREDIT
19—								
Sept. 15	523	Kerry Meadows	Salaries Expense	622	650 00			650 00
16	524	Johnson Company		✓		3750 00	75 00	3675 00
30	525	Kerry Meadows	Salaries Expense	622	650 00			650 00
30	526	Olson Company		✓		1750 00	35 00	1715 00
30			Totals		1300 00	5500 00	110 00	6690 00
					(✓)	(201)	(507)	(101)

GENERAL LEDGER

Cash   No. 101

Date	Debit	Credit	Balance
Sept. 30	22,196.50		22,196.50
30		6,690.00	15,506.50

Accounts Receivable   No. 106

Date	Debit	Credit	Balance
Sept. 30	8,125.00		8,125.00
30		2,700.00	5,425.00

Store Equipment   No. 165

Date	Debit	Credit	Balance
Sept. 30	950.00		950.00

Accounts Payable   No. 201

Date	Debit	Credit	Balance
Sept. 30		16,075.00	16,075.00
30	5,500.00		10,575.00
30	625.00		9,950.00

Rent Earned   No. 406

Date	Debit	Credit	Balance
Sept. 1		550.00	550.00
30		550.00	1,100.00

Sales   No. 413

Date	Debit	Credit	Balance
Sept. 30		8,125.00	8,125.00
30		18,450.50	26,575.50

Sales Discounts   No. 415

Date	Debit	Credit	Balance
Sept. 30	54.00		54.00

Purchases   No. 505

Date	Debit	Credit	Balance
Sept. 30	15,125.00		15,125.00

Purchases Returns & Allowances   No. 506

Date	Debit	Credit	Balance
Sept. 30		625.00	625.00

Purchases Discounts   No. 507

Date	Debit	Credit	Balance
Sept. 30		110.00	110.00

Salaries Expense   No. 622

Date	Debit	Credit	Balance
Sept. 15	650.00		650.00
30	650.00		1,300.00

ACCOUNTS PAYABLE LEDGER

Johnson Company

Date	Debit	Credit	Balance
Sept. 8		3,750.00	3,750.00
16	3,750.00		-0-
30		4,000.00	4,000.00

Olson Company

Date	Debit	Credit	Balance
Sept. 22		1,750.00	1,750.00
24		5,625.00	7,375.00
30		950.00	8,325.00
30	1,750.00		6,575.00
30	625.00		5,950.00

ACCOUNTS RECEIVABLE LEDGER

N. R. Boswell

Date	Debit	Credit	Balance
Sept. 3	1,875.00		1,875.00
13		1,875.00	-0-
24	2,250.00		2,250.00

Inez Smythe

Date	Debit	Credit	Balance
Sept. 15	1,500.00		1,500.00
30	1,675.00		3,175.00

Ted Clark

Date	Debit	Credit	Balance
Sept. 20	825.00		825.00
30		825.00	-0-

MCGUFF COMPANY
Trial Balance
September 30, 19—

Cash	$15,506.50	
Accounts receivable	5,425.00	
Store equipment	950.00	
Accounts payable		$ 9,950.00
Rent earned		1,100.00
Sales		26,575.50
Sales discounts	54.00	
Purchases	15,125.00	
Purchases returns and allowances		625.00
Purchases discounts		110.00
Salaries expense	1,300.00	
Totals	$38,360.50	$38,360.50

MCGUFF COMPANY
Schedule of Accounts Receivable
September 30, 19—

N. R. Boswell	$2,250.00
Inez Smythe	3,175.00
Total accounts receivable	$5,425.00

MCGUFF COMPANY
Schedule of Accounts Payable
September 30, 19—

Johnson Company	$4,000.00
Olson Company	5,950.00
Total accounts payable	$9,950.00

7 Accounting for Cash and the Principles of Internal Control

Learning Objective 1:

Explain the concept of liquidity and the difference between cash and cash equivalents.

Summary

The liquidity of an asset refers to how easily the asset can be converted into other types of assets or used to buy services or satisfy obligations. Cash is the most liquid asset. To increase their return, companies may invest their idle cash balances in cash equivalents. These investments are readily convertible to a known amount of cash and are purchased so close to their maturity date that their market values are relatively insensitive to interest rate changes.

Learning Objective 2:

Explain why internal control procedures are needed in a large organization and state the broad principles of internal control.

Summary

Internal control systems are designed to encourage adherence to prescribed managerial policies. In doing so, they promote efficient operations and protect assets against theft or misuse. They also help ensure that accurate and reliable accounting data are produced. Principles of good internal control include establishing clear responsibilities, maintaining adequate records, insuring assets and bonding employees, separating record-keeping and custody of assets, dividing responsibilities for related transactions, using mechanical devices whenever feasible, and performing regular independent reviews of internal control practices.

Learning Objective 3:

Describe internal control procedures used to protect cash received from cash sales, cash received through the mail, and cash disbursements.

Summary

To maintain control over cash, custody must be separated from record-keeping for cash. All cash receipts should be deposited intact in the bank on a daily basis, and all payments (except for minor petty cash payments) should be made by check. A voucher system helps maintain control over cash disbursements by ensuring that payments are made only after full documentation and approval.

Learning Objective 4:

Explain the operation of a petty cash fund and be able to prepare journal entries to record petty cash fund transactions.

Summary

The petty cashier, who should be a responsible employee, makes small payments from the petty cash fund and obtains signed receipts for the payments. The Petty Cash account is debited when the fund is established or increased in size. Petty cash disbursements are recorded with a credit to cash whenever the fund is replenished.

Learning Objective 5:

Explain why the bank balance and the book balance of cash should be reconciled and be able to prepare a reconciliation.

Summary

A bank reconciliation is produced to prove the accuracy of the depositor's and the bank's records. In completing the reconciliation, the bank statement balance is adjusted for such items as outstanding checks and unrecorded deposits made on or before the bank statement date but not reflected on the statement. The depositor's cash account balance is adjusted to the correct balance. The difference arises from such items as service charges, collections the bank has made for the depositor, and interest earned on the average checking account balance.

Learning Objective 6:

Explain how recording invoices at net amounts helps gain control over cash discounts taken, and calculate days' sales uncollected.

Summary

When the net method of recording invoices is used, missed cash discounts are reported as an expense in the income statement. In contrast, when the gross method is used, discounts taken are reported as reductions in the cost of the purchased goods. Therefore, the net method directs management's attention to instances where the company failed to take advantage of discounts. In evaluating the liquidity of a company, financial statement users may calculate days' sales uncollected.

Learning Objective 7:

Define or explain the words and phrases listed in the chapter glossary.

Summary

See Problem III.

Topical Outline

I. Cash, cash equivalents, and the concept of liquidity

   A. Cash includes currency and coins, checking accounts, some savings accounts, and items that are acceptable for deposit in those accounts.

   B. A cash equivalent is a highly liquid, short-term investment that generally meets two criteria:

      1. It is readily convertible into a known amount of cash.

      2. It is close enough to its maturity date so that its market value is relatively insensitive to interest rate changes.

   C. The liquidity of an asset refers to how easily the asset can be converted into other types of assets or be used to buy services or pay liabilities.

II. Internal control procedures—designed to protect assets from fraud and theft

   A. Seven broad principles of internal control are:

      1. Responsibilities should be clearly established.

      2. Adequate records should be maintained.

      3. Assets should be insured and employees bonded.

      4. Record-keeping and custody of assets should be separated.

      5. Responsibility for related transactions should be divided.

      6. Mechanical devices should be used whenever practicable.

      7. Regular and independent reviews should be conducted.

   B. Computers and internal control:

      1. Computers provide rapid access to large quantities of information.

      2. Computers reduce processing errors.

      3 Computers allow more extensive testing of records.

      4. Computers may limit hard evidence of processing steps.

      5. Separation of duties must be maintained.

   C. Internal control for cash should include procedures for protecting:

      1. Cash receipts

         a. Cash from cash sales.

         b. Cash received through the mail.

      2. Cash disbursements

   D. Voucher system—used to control the incurrence of obligations and disbursements of cash. With a voucher system, important business papers include:

      1. Purchase requisitions.

      2. Purchase orders.

      3. Invoices.

      4. Receiving reports.

      5. Invoice approval forms.

      6. Vouchers.

III. Accounting for cash

    A. Petty cash fund—used to avoid writing checks for small amounts

        1. Petty Cash is debited only when the fund is established or increased.

        2. Petty cash receipts are retained by the petty cashier to account for the amounts expended.

        3. When the petty cash fund is reimbursed, an entry is made to debit the expenses or other items paid for with petty cash and to credit Cash for the amount reimbursed to the petty cash fund.

    B. Cash Over and Short account—an income statement account used to record cash overages and cash shortages that result from omitted petty cash receipts and from errors in making change.

    C. Reconciling the bank balance

        1. A bank reconciliation is an analysis that explains the difference between the balance of a checking account shown in the depositor's records and the balance shown on the bank statement.

        2. Items that may cause a difference between the bank statement balance and a depositor's book balance of cash:

            a. Outstanding checks.

            b. Unrecorded deposits.

            c. Charges for services and uncollectible items.

            d. Collections made by the bank for the depositor.

            e. Errors.

        3. Steps in reconciling the bank balance:

            a. Compare deposits listed on the bank statement with deposits shown in the accounting records.

            b. Determine whether other credits on bank statement (interest, etc.) have been recorded in the books.

            c. Compare canceled checks listed on bank statement with actual checks returned with statement.

            d. Compare canceled checks listed on bank statement with checks recorded in books since last reconciliation.

            e. Compare previous month's outstanding checks with canceled checks listed on this month's bank statement.

            f. Note any unrecorded debits shown on bank statement; e.g., check printing charges, NSF checks, service charges.

            g. Prepare reconciliation.

            h. Make journal entries for any unrecorded debits or credits appearing on the bank statement.

IV. Recording purchases

    A. Gross method—purchases are recorded at the full invoice price without deducting cash discounts.

    B. Net method—purchases recorded at net amount of invoices (full invoice price less any cash discounts); provides better control over purchases discounts.

V. Days' sales uncollected

    A. Used to evaluate the liquidity of a company. Estimates how much time is likely to pass before cash receipts from credit sales will equal the amount of existing accounts receivable.

    B. Calculated as: $\dfrac{\text{Accounts receivable}}{\text{Net sales}} \times 365$

Problem I

The following statements are either true or false. Place a (T) in the parentheses before each true statement and an (F) before each false statement.

1. ( ) One of the fundamental principles of internal control states that the person who has access to or is responsible for an asset should not maintain the accounting record for that asset.

2. ( ) Procedures for controlling cash disbursements are as important as those for cash receipts.

3. ( ) When a voucher system is used, duplication of procedures among several departments is instrumental in maintaining control over cash disbursements.

4. ( ) In order to approve an invoice for payment for the purchase of assets, the accounting department of a large company should require copies of the purchase requisition, purchase order, invoice, and receiving report.

5. ( ) After the petty cash fund is established, the Petty Cash account is not debited or credited again unless the size of the fund is changed.

6. ( ) The Cash Over and Short account is usually shown on the income statement as part of miscellaneous revenues if it has a credit balance at the end of the period.

7. ( ) If 20 canceled checks are listed on the current month's bank statement, then no less than 20 checks could have been issued during the current month.

8. ( ) When the net method of recording invoices is used, cash discounts lost are reported as an expense in the income statement; when the gross method is used, cash discounts taken are deducted from purchases in the income statement.

Problem II

You are given several words, phrases, or numbers to choose from in completing each of the following statements or in answering the following questions. In each case select the one that best completes the statement or answers the question and place its letter in the answer space provided.

_____ 1. A voucher system:

    a. Permits only authorized individuals to incur obligations that will result in cash disbursements.

    b. Establishes procedures for incurring such obligations and for their verification, approval, and recording.

    c. Permits checks to be issued only in payment of properly verified, approved, and recorded obligations.

    d. Requires that every obligation be recorded at the time it is incurred and every purchase be treated as an independent transaction, complete in itself.

    e. Does all of the above.

_____ 2. Liquidity is:

    a. The portion of a corporation's equity that represents investments in the corporation by its stockholders.

    b. Cash or other assets that are reasonably expected to be realized in cash or be sold or consumed within one year or one operating cycle of the business.

    c. A characteristic of an asset indicating how easily the asset can be converted into cash or used to buy services or satisfy obligations.

    d. Obligations that are due to be paid or liquidated within one year or one operating cycle of the business.

    e. Economic benefits or resources without physical substance, the value of which stems from the privileges or rights that accrue to their owner.

_____ 3. A voucher is a:

a. Business paper used in summarizing a transaction and approving it for recording and payment.
b. Business form used within a business to ask the purchasing department of the business to buy needed items.
c. Document, prepared by a vendor, on which are listed the items sold, the sales prices, the customer's name, and the terms of sale.
d. Form used within a business to notify the proper persons of the receipt of goods ordered and of the quantities and condition of the goods.
e. Document on which the accounting department notes that it has performed each step in the process of checking an invoice and approving it for recording and payment.

_____ 4. Each of the following items would cause Brand X Sales Company's book balance of cash to differ from its bank statement balance.

A. A service charge made by the bank.
B. A check listed as outstanding on the previous month's reconciliation and that is still outstanding.
C. A customer's check returned by the bank marked "NSF."
D. A deposit which was mailed to the bank on the last day of November and is unrecorded on the November bank statement.
E. A check paid by the bank at its correct $422 amount but recorded in error in the General Journal at $442.
F. An unrecorded credit memorandum indicating the bank had collected a note receivable for Brand X Sales Company and deposited the proceeds in the company's account.
G. A check written during November and not yet paid and returned by the bank.

Which of the above items require entries on the books of Brand X Sales Company?

a. A., B., C., and E.
b. A., C., E., and F.
c. A., B., D., and F.
d. A., B., D., E., and G.
e. C., D., E., and F.

_____ 5. A company reported net sales for 19X1 and 19X2 of $560,000 and $490,000 respectively. The year-end balances of accounts receivable were $34,000 and $31,000. Days' sales uncollected for 19X2 is:

a. 6 days.
b. 20.2 days.
c. 15.8 days.
d. 23.1 days.
e. 24.2 days.

Problem III

Many of the important ideas and concepts discussed in Chapter 7 are reflected in the following list of key terms. Test your understanding of these terms by matching the appropriate definitions with the terms. Record the number identifying the most appropriate definition in the blank space next to each term.

_____ Bank reconciliation   _____ Liquidity

_____ Canceled checks   _____ Net method of recording purchases

_____ Cash equivalents   _____ Outstanding checks

_____ Cash Over and Short account   _____ Purchase order

_____ Days' sales uncollected   _____ Purchase requisition

_____ Discounts lost   _____ Receiving report

_____ Gross method of recording purchases   _____ Vendee

_____ Internal control system   _____ Vendor

_____ Invoice   _____ Voucher

_____ Invoice approval form   _____ Voucher system

_____ Liquid asset

1. A form used within the business to notify the appropriate persons that ordered goods were received and to describe the quantities and condition of the goods.

2. A characteristic of an asset that refers to how easily the asset can be converted into another type of asset or used to buy services or satisfy obligations.

3. An expense resulting from failing to take advantage of cash discounts on purchases.

4. Checks that were written (or drawn) by the depositor, deducted on the depositor's records, and sent to the payees; however, they had not reached the bank for payment and deduction before the statement date.

5. The seller of goods or services, usually a manufacturer or wholesaler.

6. An itemized statement prepared by the vendor that lists the customer's name, the items sold, the sales prices, and the terms of sale.

7. An internal business paper that is used to accumulate other papers and information needed to control the disbursement of cash and to ensure that the transaction is properly recorded.

8. A method of recording purchases at the full invoice price without deducting any cash discounts.

9. An asset, such as cash, that is easily converted into other types of assets or used to buy services or pay liabilities.

10. Checks that the bank has paid and deducted from the customer's account during the month.

11. A document on which the accounting department notes that it has performed each step in the process of checking an invoice and approving it for recording and payment.

12. A business paper used to request that the purchasing department buy the needed merchandise or other items.

13. An income statement account used to record cash overages and cash shortages arising from omitted petty cash receipts and from errors in making change.

14. Procedures adopted by a business to encourage adherence to prescribed managerial policies; in doing so, the system also promotes operational efficiencies and protects the business assets from waste, fraud, and theft, and helps ensure that accurate and reliable accounting data are produced.

15. A set of procedures designed to control the incurrence of obligations and disbursements of cash.

16. A business paper used by the purchasing department to place an order with the vendor; authorizes the vendor to ship the ordered merchandise at the stated price and terms.

17. An analysis that explains the difference between the balance of a checking account shown in the depositor's records and the balance shown on the bank statement.

18. The number of days of average credit sales volume accumulated in the accounts receivable balance, calculated as the product of 365 times the ratio of the accounts receivable balance divided by credit (or net) sales.

19. A method of recording purchases at the full invoice price less any cash discounts.

20. The buyer or purchaser of goods or services.

21. Temporary liquid investments that can be easily and quickly converted to cash.

Problem IV

Complete the following by filling in the blanks.

1. If a cashier errs while making change and gives a customer too much money back, the resulting cash shortage is recorded with a debit to an account called _____ .

2. A(n) _____ form is used by the accounting department in checking and approving an invoice for recording and payment.

3. Cash discounts offered but not taken are _____ .

4. If the size of the petty cash fund remains unchanged, the Petty Cash account _____ (is, is not) debited in the entry to replenish the petty cash fund.

5. Control of a small business is commonly gained through the direct supervision and active participation of the _____ in the affairs and activities of the business. However, as a business grows, it becomes necessary for the manager to delegate responsibilities and rely on _____ rather than personal contact in controlling the affairs and activities of the business.

6. A properly designed internal control system encourages adherence to prescribed managerial policies; and it also (a) _____
_____ ;
(b) _____
_____ ; and (c) _____
_____ .

Fundamental Accounting Principles, 14th Edition

7. A good system of internal control for cash requires a _____
   of duties so that the people responsible for handling cash and for its custody are not the same people

   who _____ . It also requires that all cash receipts be deposited

   in the bank _____ and that all payments, except petty cash

   payments, be made by _____ .

8. A bank reconciliation is prepared to account for the difference between the _____

   and the _____ .

9. An accounting system used to control the incurrence and payment of obligations requiring the

   disbursement of cash is a _____ .

10. A _____ is commonly used by a selling department to notify the
    purchasing department of items which the selling department wishes the purchasing department to
    purchase.

11. The business form commonly used by the purchasing department of a large company to order

    merchandise is called a(n) _____ .

12. Good internal control follows certain broad principles. These principles are:

    (a) Responsibilities should be clearly established, and in every situation

        _____ should be made responsible for each task.

    (b) Adequate records should be maintained since they provide an important means of protecting

        _____ .

    (c) Assets should be _____ and employees _____ .

    (d) Record-keeping for assets and _____ of assets should be separated.

    (e) Responsibility for related transactions should be _____ so that the work of
        one department or individual may act as a check on the work of others.

    (f) Mechanical devices _____ where practicable.

    (g) Regular and independent _____ of internal control procedures
        should be conducted.

13. After preparing a bank reconciliation, journal entries _____ (should, should not)
    be made to record those items listed as outstanding checks.

14. Days' sales uncollected is used in evaluating the _____ of a company.

Problem V

On November 5 of the current year Cullen Company drew Check No. 23 for $50 to establish a petty cash fund.

1. Give the general journal entry to record the establishment of the fund.

DATE	ACCOUNT TITLES AND EXPLANATION	P.R.	DEBIT	CREDIT

After making a payment from petty cash on November 25, the petty cashier noted that there was only $2.50 cash remaining in the fund. The cashier prepared the following list of expenditures from the fund and requested that the fund be replenished.

Nov.	9	Express freight on merchandise purchased	$ 9.75
	12	Miscellaneous expense to clean office	10.00
	15	Office supplies	3.50
	18	Delivery of merchandise to customer	8.00
	23	Miscellaneous expense for collect telegram	3.25
	25	Express freight on merchandise purchased	13.00

Check No. 97 in the amount of $47.50 was drawn to replenish the fund.

2. In the General Journal below give the entry to record the check replenishing the petty cash fund.

DATE	ACCOUNT TITLES AND EXPLANATION	P.R.	DEBIT	CREDIT

Problem VI

Information about the following eight items is available to prepare Verde Company's December 31 bank reconciliation.

Two checks (1) No. 453 and (2) No. 457 were outstanding on November 30. Check No. 457 was returned with the December bank statement but Check No. 453 was not. (3) Check No. 478, written on December 26, was not returned with the canceled checks; and (4) Check No. 480 for $96 was incorrectly entered in the Cash Disbursements Journal and posted as though it were for $69. (5) A deposit placed in the bank's night depository after banking hours on November 30 appeared on the December bank statement, but (6) one placed there after hours on December 31 did not. (7) Enclosed with the December bank statement was a debit memorandum for a bank service charge and (8) a check received from a customer and deposited on December 27 but returned by the bank marked "Not Sufficient Funds."

1. If an item in the above list should not appear on the December 31 bank reconciliation, ignore it. However, if an item should appear, enter its number in a set of parentheses to show where it should be added or subtracted in preparing the reconciliation.

VERDE COMPANY
Bank Reconciliation
December 31, 19—

Book balance of cash	$X,XXX	Bank statement balance	$X,XXX
Add:		Add:	
( )		( )	
( )		( )	
( )		( )	
Deduct:		Deduct:	
( )		( )	
( )		( )	
( )		( )	
Reconciled balance	$X,XXX	Reconciled balance	$X,XXX

2. Certain of the above items require entries on Verde Company's books. Place the numbers of these items within the following parentheses:

(   ), (   ), (   ), (   ), (   ), (   )

Problem VII

On May 8 a company that records purchases at net amounts received a shipment of merchandise having a $3,750 invoice price. Attached to the merchandise was the invoice, which was dated May 6, terms 2/10, n/60, FOB the vendor's warehouse. The vendor, Vee Company, had prepaid the shipping charges on the goods, $125, adding the amount to the invoice and bringing its total to $3,875. The invoice was recorded and filed in error for payment on May 26. Give in general journal form the entries to record the (1) purchase, (2) discovery on May 26 of the discount lost, and (3) payment of the invoice on July 5. Do not give explanations but skip a line between entries.

DATE	ACCOUNT TITLES AND EXPLANATION	P.R.	DEBIT	CREDIT

Problem VIII

1. The ABC Company records all purchases at gross amounts. Give in general journal form the entries to record the following transactions (do not give explanations but skip a line between entries):

   June 1   Received shipment of merchandise having $2,000 invoice price, terms 2/10, n/30.

   June 2   Received shipment of merchandise having $500 invoice price, terms 1/10, n/60.

   June 7   Paid for merchandise which was received on June 1.

   July 30   Paid for merchandise which was received on June 2.

DATE	ACCOUNT TITLES AND EXPLANATION	P.R.	DEBIT	CREDIT

2. Show the appropriate general journal entries for the ABC Company if they had recorded purchases at net amounts (do not give explanations but skip a line between entries):

DATE	ACCOUNT TITLES AND EXPLANATION	P.R.	DEBIT	CREDIT

Problem IX

The bank statement dated September 30, 19X1, for the Smith Company showed a balance of $2,876.35 which differs from the $1,879.50 book balance of cash on that date. In attempting to reconcile the difference, the accountant noted the following facts:

1) The bank recorded a service fee of $15 which was not recorded on the books of Smith Company.

2) A deposit of $500 was made on the last day of the month but was not recorded by the bank.

3) A check for $176 had been recorded on the Smith Company books as $167. The bank paid the correct amount.

4) A check was written during September but has not been processed by the bank. The amount was $422.85.

5) A check for $1,000 is still outstanding from August.

6) A check for $100 deposited by Smith Company was returned marked "Not Sufficient Funds."

7) A credit memorandum stated that the bank collected a note receivable of $200 for Smith Company and charged Smith a $2 collection fee. Smith Company had not previously recorded the collection.

Prepare, in good form, a bank reconciliation which shows the correct cash balance on September 30, 19X1.

Solutions for Chapter 7

Problem I

1. T	5. T
2. T	6. T
3. F	7. F
4. T	8. T

Problem II

1. E
2. C
3. A
4. B
5. D

Problem III

Bank reconciliation 17	Liquidity 2
Canceled checks 10	Net method of recording purchases 19
Cash equivalents 21	Outstanding checks 4
Cash Over and Short account 13	Purchase order 16
Days' sales uncollected 18	Purchase requisition 12
Discounts lost 3	Receiving report 1
Gross method of recording purchases 8	Vendee 20
Internal control system 14	Vendor 5
Invoice 6	Voucher 7
Invoice approval form 11	Voucher system 15
Liquid asset 9	

Problem IV

1. Cash Over and Short

2. invoice approval

3. discounts lost

4. is not

5. owner-manager, a system of internal control

6. (a) promotes operational efficiencies; (b) protects the business assets from waste, fraud, and theft; and (c) ensures accurate and reliable accounting data

7. separation, keep the cash records, intact each day, check

8. book balance of cash, bank statement balance

9. voucher system

10. purchase requisition

11. purchase order

12. (a) one person; (b) assets; (c) insured, bonded; (d) custody; (e) divided; (f) should be used; (g) reviews

13. should not

14. liquidity

Problem V

1. Nov. 5   Petty Cash 50.00
            Cash 50.00
            Established a petty cash fund.

2. Nov. 25   Transportation-In 22.75
            Miscellaneous Expenses 13.25
            Office Supplies 3.50
            Delivery Expense 8.00
            Cash 47.50
            Reimbursed the petty cash fund.

Problem VI

1. Book balance of cash .... \$X,XXX   Bank statement balance .... \$X,XXX
      Add: Add:
          (   )   (6)
      Deduct: Deduct:
          (4)   (1)
          (7)   (3)
          (8)   (   )

2. (4), (7), (8)

Problem VII

May 8   Purchases 3,675.00
          Transportation-In 125.00
          Accounts Payable—Vee Company 3,800.00
          \$3,750 − (\$3,750 × .02) = \$3,675

     26   Discounts Lost 75.00
          Accounts Payable—Vee Company 75.00

July 5   Accounts Payable—Vee Company 3,875.00
          Cash 3,875.00

Problem VIII

1.	June	1	Purchases	2,000.00	
			Accounts Payable		2,000.00
		2	Purchases	500.00	
			Accounts Payable		500.00
		7	Accounts Payable	2,000.00	
			Purchases Discounts		40.00
			Cash		1,960.00
	July	30	Accounts Payable	500.00	
			Cash		500.00
2.	June	1	Purchases ($2,000 × 98%)	1,960.00	
			Accounts Payable		1,960.00
		2	Purchases ($500 × 99%)	495.00	
			Accounts Payable		495.00
		7	Accounts Payable	1,960.00	
			Cash		1,960.00
	July	30	Discounts Lost	5.00	
			Accounts Payable		5.00
		30	Accounts Payable	500.00	
			Cash		500.00

Problem IX

SMITH COMPANY
Bank Reconciliation
September 30, 19X1

Book balance of cash	$1,879.50	Bank statement balance		$2,876.35
Add:		Add:		
Proceeds of note less				
collection fee	198.00	Deposit on 9/30/X1		500.00
	$2,077.50			$3,376.35
Deduct:		Deduct:		
NSF check $100.00		Outstanding checks:		
Service fee 15.00		August $1,000.00		
Recording error 9.00	124.00	September 422.85	1,422.85	
Reconciled balance	$1,953.50	Reconciled balance		$1,953.50

8 Short-Term Investments and Receivables

Learning Objective 1:

Prepare journal entries to account for short-term investments and explain how fair (market) value gains and losses on such investments are reported.

Summary

Short-term investments are recorded at cost; dividends and interest on the investments are recorded in appropriate income statement accounts. On the balance sheet, investments in securities held to maturity are reported at cost; investments in trading securities and securities available for sale are reported at their fair values. Unrealized gains and losses on trading securities are included in income, but unrealized gains and losses on securities available for sale are reported as a separate stockholders' equity item.

Learning Objective 2:

Prepare entries to account for credit card sales.

Summary

When credit card receipts are deposited in a bank account, the credit card expense is recorded at the time of the deposit. When credit card receipts must be submitted to the credit card company for payment, Accounts Receivable is debited for the sales amount. Then, credit card expense is recorded when cash is received from the credit card company. However, any unrecorded credit card expense should be accrued at the end of each accounting period.

Learning Objective 3:

Prepare entries to account for transactions with credit customers, including accounting for bad debts under the allowance method and the direct write-off method.

Summary

Under the allowance method, bad debts expense is recorded with an adjustment at the end of each accounting period that debits the expense and credits the Allowance for Doubtful Accounts. The amount of the adjustment is determined by focusing on either (a) the income statement relationship between bad debts expense and credit sales or (b) the balance sheet relationship between accounts receivable and the Allowance for Doubtful Accounts. The latter approach may involve using a simple percentage relationship or aging the accounts. Uncollectible accounts are written off with a debit to the Allowance for Doubtful Accounts. The direct write-off method charges Bad Debts Expense when accounts are written off as uncollectible. This method is suitable only when the amount of bad debts expense is immaterial.

Learning Objective 4:

Calculate the interest on promissory notes and prepare entries to record the receipt of promissory notes and their payment or dishonor.

Summary

Interest rates are typically stated in annual terms. When a note's time to maturity is more or less than one year, the amount of interest on the note must be determined by expressing the time as a fraction of one year and multiplying the note's principal by that fraction and the annual interest rate. Dishonored notes are credited to Notes Receivable and debited to Accounts Receivable and to the account of the maker.

Learning Objective 5:

Explain how receivables can be converted into cash before they are due and calculate accounts receivable turnover.

Summary

To obtain cash from receivables before they are due, a company may sell accounts receivable to a factor, who charges a factoring fee. Also, a company may borrow money by signing a note payable that is secured by pledging the accounts receivable. Notes receivable may be discounted at a bank, with or without recourse. The full-disclosure principle requires companies to disclose the amount of accounts receivable that have been pledged and the contingent liability for notes discounted with recourse.

Learning Objective 6:

Define or explain the words and phrases listed in the chapter glossary.

Summary

See Problem III.

Topical Outline

I. Short-term investments

    A. Short-term investments must be readily convertible into cash and held as a source of cash to satisfy the needs of current operations. They are classified as current assets on the balance sheet.

    B. Recorded at cost, which includes any commissions paid.

    C. Reporting and accounting for short-term investments.

        1. Investments in securities held to maturity—investments in debt securities that the owner positively intends and has the ability to hold until maturity.

            a. Reported at cost.

        2. Investments in trading securities—investments in debt and equity securities that the owner actively manages, so that frequent purchases and sales generally are made with the objective of generating profits on short-term differences in price.

            a. Reported at fair (market) value.

            b. Fair value gains and losses are reported on the income statement and closed to Retained Earnings.

        3. Investments in securities available for sale—investments in debt and equity securities that do not qualify as investments in trading securities or as investments in securities held to maturity.

            a. Reported at fair (market) value.

            b. Fair value gains and losses are reported in the stockholders' equity section of the balance sheet.

II. Credit card sales

    A. Receipts from some credit card sales are deposited like checks into a business's bank account for immediate cash credit.

    B. Receipts from other credit card sales are sent to the credit card company for payment. The business has an account receivable from the credit card company until payment is received.

III. Subsidiary Accounts Receivable Ledger

    A. Accounts Receivable account in General Ledger is controlling account for subsidiary ledger.

    B. A separate account for each customer is maintained in the Accounts Receivable Ledger.

IV. Bad debts—accounts receivable from customers that are not collected

    A. A necessary expense associated with selling on credit.

    B. Bad debts expense should be matched with the sales that resulted in the bad debts (matching principle).

    C. Methods of accounting for bad debts

        1. Allowance method—at the end of each accounting period, bad debts expense is estimated and recorded. Accounts receivable are reported at their estimated realizable value by crediting a contra account called the Allowance for Doubtful Accounts.

        2. Direct write-off method—uncollectible accounts are written off directly to Bad Debts Expense.

            a. Generally considered inferior to the allowance method because of the potential for mismatching revenues and expenses.

            b. May be used if bad debts expenses are very small and the effects on the financial statements are unimportant to users (materiality principle).

D. Methods of estimating bad debts expense

1. Income statement approach—bad debts expense is calculated as a percentage of credit sales.

2. Balance sheet approach—desired credit balance in Allowance for Doubtful Accounts is calculated:

   a. As a percentage of outstanding receivables (simplified approach).

   b. By aging of accounts receivable.

E. Recovery of bad debts

1. Reinstate customer's account (reverse original write-off).

2. Record collection of reinstated account.

V. Installment accounts and notes receivable

A. Installment accounts receivable—accounts receivable that allow the customer to make periodic payments over several months and that typically earn interest for the seller.

B. Note receivable—a written document that promises payment and is signed by the customer.

1. Promissory notes are notes payable to the maker of the note and notes receivable to the payee of the note.

2. Notes receivable are generally preferred by creditors over accounts receivable.

C. Calculating interest

$$\text{Principal of note} \times \text{Annual rate of interest} \times \text{Time of note expressed in years} = \text{Interest}$$

D. Accounting for notes receivable

1. Record receipt of note.

2. Record end-of-period adjustment for accrued interest.

3. Record receipt of note payments.

4. If a note is dishonored, amount of note should be removed from the Notes Receivable account and charged back to an account receivable from its maker.

VI. Converting receivables into cash before due

A. Selling accounts receivable

1. Risk of bad debts passes from seller to the factor (buyer of the accounts).

2. Factoring fee—fee charged by the factor to the seller.

B. Pledging accounts receivable as security for loan

1. Risk of bad debts is not passed to the lender. Borrower retains ownership of receivables. If borrower defaults on loan, creditor has right to be paid from cash receipts of accounts receivable collected.

2. Financial statement disclosure required.

C. Discounting notes receivable

1. With recourse—if the original maker of note defaults, the original payee must pay.

a. A company that discounts the note has a contingent liability—an obligation to make a future payment if and only if an uncertain future event actually occurs.

b. If the discounting transaction is considered to be a loan, the cost of discounting is debited to Interest Expense.

c. If the discounting transaction is considered to be a sale, the cost of discounting is debited to Loss on Sale of Notes.

d. Financial statement disclosure required.

2. Without recourse—no contingent liability. Bank assumes the risk of a bad debt loss.

VII. Full-disclosure principle—requires financial statements to present all relevant information about the operations and financial position of the entity. Items to be disclosed include:

A. Contingent liabilities.

B. Long-term commitments under contracts.

C. Accounting methods used.

VIII. Accounts receivable turnover

A. Indicates how often the company converted its average accounts receivable balance into cash during the year.

B. Calculated as: $\dfrac{\text{Net sales}}{\text{Average accounts receivable}}$

Problem I

The following statements are either true or false. Place a (T) in the parentheses before each true statement and an (F) before each false statement.

1. ( ) Short-term investments are classified as current assets on the balance sheet.

2. ( ) Investments in securities that do not mature within one year or the current operating cycle of the business can be classified as current assets on the balance sheet if they are marketable.

3. ( ) A stock quotation of 14-1/8 means $14.125 per share.

4. ( ) A short-term investment in a security available for sale is reported on the balance sheet at cost.

5. ( ) A fair value gain on a short-term investment in a security available for sale is reported in the stockholders' equity section of the balance sheet, whereas a fair value gain on a short-term investment in a trading security is reported on the income statement.

6. ( ) A short-term investment in a security held to maturity is reported on the balance sheet at its fair (market) value.

7. ( ) If cash from credit card sales is received immediately when the credit card receipts are deposited at the bank, the credit card expense is recorded at the time the sale is recorded.

8. ( ) Businesses with credit customers must maintain a separate account for each customer.

9. ( ) After all entries are posted, the sum of the balances in the Accounts Receivable Ledger should be equal to the balance of the Accounts Receivable account in the General Ledger.

10. ( ) Under the allowance method of accounting for bad debts, accounts receivable are reported on the balance sheet at the amount of cash proceeds expected from their collection.

11. ( ) At the time an adjusting entry to record estimated bad debts expense is made, the credit side of the entry is to Accounts Receivable.

12. ( ) When an account deemed uncollectible is written off against Allowance for Doubtful Accounts, the estimated realizable amount of Accounts Receivable is decreased.

13. ( ) The income statement approach to estimating bad debts is based on the idea that some percentage of credit sales will be uncollectible.

14. ( ) The balance sheet approach to estimating bad debts is based on the idea that some particular percentage of a company's credit sales will become uncollectible.

15. ( ) Aging of accounts receivable requires the examination of each account in the accounts receivable ledger.

16. ( ) A 90-day note, dated August 17, matures on November 16.

17. ( ) Although the direct write-off method of accounting for bad debts usually mismatches revenues and expenses, it may be allowed in cases where bad debt losses are immaterial in relation to total net sales and net income.

18. ( ) When a note receivable is discounted with recourse and the transaction is considered to be a loan, the cost of discounting is charged to Loss on Sale of Notes.

19. ( ) When a note receivable is discounted with recourse, the company that discounts the note has a contingent liability.

20. ( ) A company that pledges its accounts receivable as security for a loan should disclose the fact in a footnote to the financial statements.

Problem II

You are given several words, phrases, or numbers to choose from in completing each of the following statements or in answering the following questions. In each case select the one that best completes the statement or answers the question and place its letter in the answer space provided.

_____ 1. On June 12, Cookie Company purchased 400 shares of Photograph Company common stock at 12-1/8 plus a 1% brokerage fee as a short-term investment. What is the general journal entry to record the transaction?

   a. Short-Term Investments 4,851.00
        Cash 4,851.00
   b. Cash 4,365.00
        Short-Term Investments 4,365.00
   c. Short-Term Investments 4,898.50
        Cash 4,898.50
   d. Cash 4,801.50
        Short-Term Investments 4,801.50
   e. Short-Term Investments 4,365.00
        Cash 4,365.00

_____ 2. The cost and market values of Company B's short-term investments on December 31, 19X1, follow:

	Cost	Market
Securities held to maturity	$30,000	$28,000
Trading securities	34,000	32,500
Securities available for sale	28,000	31,000

What dollar amount should be reported on Company B's December 31, 19X1, balance sheet for each of the three types of short-term investments?

   a. $30,000; $34,000; $28,000.
   b. $30,000; $32,500; $31,000.
   c. $28,000; $32,500; $31,000.
   d. $28,000; $34,000; $28,000.
   e. $28,000; $32,500; $28,000.

_____ 3. Orion Company has decided to write off the account of Jack Irwin against the Allowance for Doubtful Accounts. The $2,100 balance in Irwin's account originated with a credit sale in July of last year. What is the general journal entry to record this write-off?

   a. Allowance for Doubtful Accounts 2,100
        Accounts Receivable—Jack Irwin 2,100
   b. Accounts Receivable 2,100
        Allowance for Doubtful Accounts 2,100
   c. Bad Debts Expense 2,100
        Allowance for Doubtful Accounts 2,100
   d. Accounts Receivable 2,100
        Accounts Receivable—Jack Irwin 2,100
   e. Bad Debts Expense 2,100
        Accounts Receivable 2,100

_____ 4. Hitech Corporation had credit sales of $3,000,000 in 19X1. Before recording the December 31, 19X1, adjustments, the company's Allowance for Doubtful Accounts had a credit balance of $1,400. A schedule of the December 31, 19X1, accounts receivable by age is summarized as follows:

December 31, 19X1 Accounts Receivable	Age of Accounts Receivable	Uncollectible Percent Expected
$285,000	Not due	1.5
87,000	1–45 days past due	8.2
34,000	46–90 days past due	37.0
8,000	over 90 days past due	70.0

Calculate the amount that should appear on the December 31, 19X1, balance sheet as allowance for doubtful accounts.

a. $28,189.
b. $ 5,600.
c. $25,314.
d. $30,989.
e. $29,589.

_____ 5. Based on the information given in problem 4, what is the general journal entry to record bad debts expense for 19X1?

a. Debit Bad Debts Expense; credit Allowance for Doubtful Accounts.
b. Debit Accounts Receivable; credit Allowance for Doubtful Accounts.
c. Debit Bad Debts Expense; credit Accounts Receivable.
d. Debit Allowance for Doubtful Accounts; credit Bad Debts Expense.
e. Debit Accounts Receivable; credit Bad Debts Expense.

_____ 6. MBC Company discounts a $25,000 note receivable, with recourse, at a cost of $250 and the transaction is considered to be a loan. MBC's entry to record the transaction would include the following:

a. $25,250 debit to Cash.
b. $250 debit to Interest Expense.
c. $250 debit to Loss on Sale of Notes.
d. $24,750 credit to Notes Receivable.
e. None of the above.

_____ 7. Westing Company had net sales of $500,000 and $400,000 for 19X2 and 19X1, respectively. Accounts receivable at December 31, 19X2 and 19X1, were $45,000 and $55,000. What is Westing's accounts receivable turnover for 19X2?

a. 11.1 times.
b. 10.0 times.
c. 20.0 times.
d. 9.0 times.
e. None of the above.

Problem III

Many of the important ideas and concepts discussed in Chapter 8 are reflected in the following list of key terms. Test your understanding of these terms by matching the appropriate definitions with the terms. Record the number identifying the most appropriate definition in the blank space next to each term.

_____ Accounts Receivable Ledger

_____ Accounts receivable turnover

_____ Aging accounts receivable

_____ Allowance for Doubtful Accounts

_____ Allowance method of accounting for bad debts

_____ Bad debts

_____ Contingent liability

_____ Controlling account

_____ Direct write-off method of accounting for bad debts

_____ Dishonoring a note

_____ Full-disclosure principle

_____ General Ledger

_____ Installment accounts receivable

_____ Interest

_____ Investments in securities available for sale

_____ Investments in securities held to maturity

_____ Investments in trading securities

_____ Maker of a note

_____ Materiality principle

_____ Maturity date of a note

_____ Payee of a note

_____ Principal of a note

_____ Promissory note

_____ Realizable value

_____ Short-term investments

_____ Subsidiary ledger

_____ Temporary investments

_____ Unrealized holding gain

_____ Unrealized holding loss

1. A measure of how long it takes a company to collect its accounts, calculated by dividing credit sales (or net sales) by the average accounts receivable balance.

2. One who signs a note and promises to pay it at maturity.

3. Collection of accounts (other than general ledger accounts) that contains the details underlying the balance of a controlling account in the General Ledger.

4. The accounting principle that requires financial statements (including the footnotes) to contain all relevant information about the operations and financial position of the entity; it also requires that the information be presented in an understandable manner.

5. An accounting procedure that (1) estimates and reports bad debts expense from credit sales during the period of the sales, and (2) reports accounts receivable at the amount of cash proceeds that is expected from their collection (their estimated realizable value).

6. An obligation to make a future payment if, and only if, an uncertain future event actually occurs.

7. Another name for _short-term investments._

8. A method that makes no attempt to estimate uncollectible accounts or bad debts expense at the end of each period; instead, an account is found to be uncollectible, it is written off directly to Bad Debts Expense; this method is generally considered to be inferior to the allowance method.

9. An increase in the fair (market) value of a security that has not yet been confirmed by the sale of the security.

10. The idea that the requirements of an accounting principle may be ignored if the effect on the financial statements is unimportant to their users.

11. Accounts receivable from customers that are not collected; the amount is an expense of selling on credit.

12. Accounts receivable that allow the customer to make periodic payments over several months and that typically earn interest for the seller.

13. The expected proceeds from converting assets into cash.

14. Investments in debt and equity securities that the owner actively manages, so that frequent purchases and sales generally are made with the objective of generating profits on short-term differences in price.

15. A contra asset account with a balance equal to the estimated amount of accounts receivable that will be uncollectible.

16. The date on which a note and any interest are due and payable.

17. A process of classifying accounts receivable by how long they have been outstanding for the purpose of estimating the amount of uncollectible accounts.

18. A supplementary record (also called a subsidiary ledger) having an account for each customer.

19. A general ledger account with a balance that is always equal to the sum of the balances in a related subsidiary ledger.

20. Investments that can be converted into cash quickly (but less quickly than cash equivalents), and that management intends to sell as a source of cash to satisfy the needs of current operations; short-term investments include such things as government or corporate debt obligations and marketable equity securities.

21. Investments in debt and equity securities that do not qualify as investments in trading securities or as investments in securities held to maturity.

22. The ledger that contains all the financial statement accounts of an organization.

23. An unconditional written promise to pay a definite sum of money on demand or at a fixed or determinable future date.

24. The charge assessed for the use of money.

25. The amount that the signer of a promissory note agrees to pay back when it matures, not including the interest.

26. Failure by a promissory note's maker to pay the amount due at maturity.

27. Investments in debt securities that the owner positively intends and has the ability to hold until maturity.

28. A decrease in the fair (market) value of a security that has not yet been confirmed by the sale of the security.

29. The one to whom a promissory note is made payable.

Problem IV

On December 12, Lark Company received from Guy Hall, a customer, $300 in cash and a $1,500, 12%, 60-day note dated December 11 in granting a time extension on Hall's past-due account. On December 31, Lark Company recorded the accrued interest on the note, and Guy Hall paid the note and its interest on the following February 9. Complete the general journal entries to record these transactions.

DATE	ACCOUNT TITLES AND EXPLANATION	P.R.	DEBIT	CREDIT
Dec. 12				
	Received cash and a note in granting a time extension			
	on a past-due account.			
31				
	To record accrued interest on a note receivable.			
Feb. 9				
	Received payment of a note and interest.			

Problem V

On March 1 Lark Company accepted a $1,200, 12%, 60-day note dated that day from a customer, Mary Dale, in granting a time extension on the customer's past-due account. When Lark Company presented the note for payment on April 30, it was dishonored, and on December 20 Lark Company wrote off the debt as uncollectible. Present entries to record the dishonor and the write-off against the company's Allowance for Doubtful Accounts.

DATE	ACCOUNT TITLES AND EXPLANATION	P.R.	DEBIT	CREDIT
Apr. 30				
	To charge the account of Mary Dale for her			
	dishonored $1,200, 12%, 60-day note.			
Dec. 20				
	To write off the uncollectible note of Mary Dale.			

Problem VI

On April 2 Lark Company received from Sam Fox, a customer, a $1,000, 12%, 60-day note dated that day in granting a time extension on his past-due account. Lark Company held the note until April 26 and then discounted it, with recourse, at its bank at a cost of $25. The transaction was considered to be a loan. Complete the following entries for this note.

DATE	ACCOUNT TITLES AND EXPLANATION	P.R.	DEBIT	CREDIT
Apr. 2				
	Received a note in granting a time extension on a			
	past-due account.			
26				
	Discounted the Sam Fox note.			

Problem VII

Hailey Company had no short-term investments prior to 19X1. The following transactions involving short-term investments available for sale occurred during 19X1:

Mar. 1 Purchased 500 shares of Abco common stock at 40-3/4 plus a $200 brokerage fee.

June 20 Purchased 1,000 shares of Carr common stock at 10-1/2 plus a $100 brokerage fee.

Nov. 3 Purchased 600 shares of TCY common stock at 20-1/4 plus a $120 brokerage fee.

On December 31, 19X1, the market prices of the securities held by Hailey were: Abco, 48-1/2; Carr, 9-3/4; and TCY, 22-1/2.

Prepare journal entries to record the preceding transactions. Also prepare an adjusing entry, if necessary, to record the fair value adjustment of the short-term investments.

DATE	ACCOUNT TITLES AND EXPLANATION	P.R.	DEBIT	CREDIT

Problem VIII

Marin Company uses the allowance method in accounting for bad debt losses, and over the past several years it has experienced an average loss equal to one fourth of 1% of its credit sales. During 19X1 the company sold $928,000 of merchandise on credit, including a $98 credit sale to Gus Bell on March 5, 19X1. The $98 had not been paid by the year's end.

1. If at the end of 19X1 Marin Company, in providing for estimated bad debt losses, assumes history will

    repeat, it will provide an allowance for 19X1 estimated bad debts equal to _____ % of its $928,000 of 19X1 charge sales; and the adjusting entry to record the allowance will appear as follows: (Complete the following entry.)

DATE	ACCOUNT TITLES AND EXPLANATION	P.R.	DEBIT	CREDIT
19X1				
Dec. 31				
	To record estimated bad debts.			

2. The debit of the foregoing entry is to the expense account, _____ _____ , which is closed to the _____ account at the end of the accounting period, just as any other expense account is closed.

3. The effect of the foregoing adjusting entry on the 19X1 income statement of Marin Company is to cause an estimated amount of bad debts expense to be deducted from the $928,000 of revenue from 19X1 charge sales. This complies with the accounting principle of _____ _____ .

4. The credit of the foregoing adjusting entry is to the contra account _____ _____ . On the December 31, 19X1, balance sheet the balance of this contra account is subtracted from the balance of the _____ account to show the amount that is expected to be realized from the accounts receivable.

5. On March 31, 19X2, the Accounts Receivable controlling account and the Allowance for Doubtful Accounts account of Marin Company had the following balances:

Accounts Receivable		Allowance for Doubtful Accounts	
Mar. 31 65,625			Mar. 31 4,475

A balance sheet which was prepared on March 31, 19X2, would show that Marin Company expects to collect $ _____ of its accounts receivable.

6. On April 1, 19X2, Marin Company decided the $98 account of Gus Bell (sale made on March 5 of the previous year) was uncollectible and wrote it off as a bad debt. (Complete the entry and post to the above T-accounts the portions affecting the accounts.)

DATE	ACCOUNT TITLES AND EXPLANATION	P.R.	DEBIT	CREDIT
19X2				
Apr. 1				
	To write off the account of Gus Bell.			

7. If a balance sheet was prepared immediately after the entry writing off the uncollectible account of Gus

Bell was posted, it would show that Marin Company expected to collect $ _____

of its accounts receivable. Consequently, the write-off _____ (did, did not) affect the net balance sheet amount of accounts receivable. Likewise, the entry writing off the account did not record an expense because the expense was anticipated and recorded in the

_____ entry made on December 31, 19X1, the year of the sale.

Problem IX

Pell Company sells almost exclusively for cash, but it does make a few small charge sales, and it also occasionally has a small bad debt loss which it accounts for by the direct write-off method.

1. Give below the entry made by Pell Company on February 5 to write off the $55 uncollectible account of Joan Bond (the goods were sold during the previous period.)

DATE	ACCOUNT TITLES AND EXPLANATION	P.R.	DEBIT	CREDIT
Feb. 5				

2. Writing off the foregoing bad debt directly to the Bad Debts Expense account violates the accounting

principle of _____ .

However, due to the accounting principle of _____
the direct write-off is permissible in this case because the company's bad debt losses are very small in relation to its sales.

Problem X

A company that ages its accounts receivable and increases its allowance for doubtful accounts to an amount sufficient to provide for estimated bad debts had a $75 debit balance in its Allowance for Doubtful Accounts account on December 31. If on that date it estimated that $1,800 of its accounts receivable were uncollectible,

it should make a year-end adjusting entry crediting $ _____ to its Allowance for Doubtful Accounts account.

Problem XI

Pierce Company allows its customers to use two credit cards: the University National Bank credit card and the Community Credit Card. Using the information given below, prepare general journal entries for Pierce Company to record the following credit card transactions:

a) University National Bank charges a 3% service fee for sales on its credit card. As a commercial customer of the bank, Pierce Company receives immediate credit when it makes its daily deposit of sales receipts.

   May 2   Sold merchandise for $525 to customers who used the University National Bank credit card.

DATE	ACCOUNT TITLES AND EXPLANATION	P.R.	DEBIT	CREDIT

b) Community Credit Card Company charges 4% of sales for use of its card. Pierce Company submits accumulated sales receipts to Community Company and is paid within thirty days.

   May 3   Sold merchandise for $675 to customers using the Community Credit Card. Submitted receipts to Community Company for payment.
      30   Received amount due from Community Credit Card Company.

DATE	ACCOUNT TITLES AND EXPLANATION	P.R.	DEBIT	CREDIT

Solutions for Chapter 8

Problem I

1.	T	11.	F
2.	T	12.	F
3.	T	13.	T
4.	F	14.	F
5.	T	15.	T
6.	F	16.	F
7.	T	17.	T
8.	T	18.	F
9.	T	19.	T
10.	T	20.	T

Problem II

1.	C
2.	B
3.	A
4.	E
5.	A
6.	B
7.	B

Problem III

Accounts Receivable Ledger 18
Accounts receivable turnover 1
Aging accounts receivable 17
Allowance for Doubtful Accounts 15
Allowance method of accounting
 for bad debts 5
Bad debts 11
Contingent liability 6
Controlling account 19
Direct write-off method of
 accounting for bad debts 8
Dishonoring a note 26
Full-disclosure principle 4
General Ledger 22
Installment accounts receivable 12
Interest 24

Investments in securities available for sale ... 21
Investments in securities held to maturity 27
Investments in trading securities 14
Maker of a note 2
Materiality principle 10
Maturity date of a note 16
Payee of a note 29
Principal of a note 25
Promissory note 23
Realizable value 13
Short-term investments 20
Subsidiary ledger 3
Temporary investments .... 7 or 20
Unrealized holding gain 9
Unrealized holding loss 28

Problem IV

Dec. 12	Cash		300.00	
	Notes Receivable		1,500.00	
	Accounts Receivable—Guy Hall			1,800.00
31	Interest Receivable ($1,500 × .12 × 20/360)		10.00	
	Interest Earned			10.00
Feb. 9	Cash		1,530.00	
	Interest Receivable			10.00
	Interest Earned			20.00
	Notes Receivable			1,500.00

Problem V

Apr. 30	Accounts Receivable—Mary Dale	1,224.00	
	Interest Earned		24.00
	Notes Receivable		1,200.00
Dec. 20	Allowance for Doubtful Accounts	1,224.00	
	Accounts Receivable—Mary Dale		1,224.00

Problem VI

Apr. 2	Notes Receivable	1,000.00	
	Accounts Receivable—Sam Fox		1,000.00
26	Cash	980.00	
	Interest Expense	20.00	
	Notes Receivable		1,000.00

Problem VII

Mar. 1	Short-Term Investments	20,575.00	
	Cash [(500 x $40.75) + $200]		20,575.00
	Purchased 500 shares of Abco.		
June 20	Short-Term Investments	10,600.00	
	Cash [(1,000 x $10.50) + $100]		10,600.00
	Purchased 1,000 shares of Carr.		
Nov. 3	Short-Term Investments	12,270.00	
	Cash [(600 x $20.25) + $120]		12,270.00
	Purchased 600 shares of TCY.		
Dec. 31	Short-Term Investments, Fair Value Adjustment	4,055.00	
	Unrealized Holding Gain (Loss)		4,055.00
	To reflect fair values of short-term investments		
	in securities held for sale.		

Short-Term Investments in Securities Available for Sale	Costs	*Fair (Market) Values*
Abco	$20,575	$24,250
Carr	10,600	9,750
TCY	12,270	13,500
Total	$43,445	$47,500

$47,500 − $43,445 = $4,055

Problem VIII

1. one fourth of 1%, or .25%

    Dec. 31 Bad Debts Expense 2,320.00
                  Allowance for Doubtful Accounts 2,320.00

2. Bad Debts Expense, Income Summary

3. matching revenues and expenses

4. Allowance for Doubtful Accounts, Accounts Receivable

5. $61,150

6. Apr. 1   Allowance for Doubtful Accounts 98.00
               Accounts Receivable—Gus Bell 98.00

Accounts Receivable				Allowance for Doubtful Accounts	
Mar. 31	65,625				Mar. 31	4,475
		Apr. 1	98	Apr. 1	98	

7. $61,150, did not, adjusting

Problem IX

1. Feb. 5 Bad Debts Expense 55.00
             Accounts Receivable—Joan Bond 55.00

2. matching revenues and expenses, materiality

Problem X

$1,875

Problem XI

a) May 2 Cash 509.25
               Credit Card Expense ($525 × 0.03) 15.75
               Sales 525.00

b) May 3 Accounts Receivable—Community Company 675.00
               Sales 675.00

        30 Cash 648.00
               Credit Card Expense ($675 × 0.04) 27.00
               Accounts Receivable—Community Company 675.00

9 Inventories and Cost of Goods Sold

Learning Objective 1:

Describe (a) how the matching principle relates to accounting for merchandise, (b) the types of items that should be included in merchandise inventory, and (c) the elements that make up the cost of merchandise.

Summary

The allocation of the cost of goods available for sale between cost of goods sold and ending inventory is an accounting application of the *matching principle*. Merchandise inventory should include all goods that are owned by the business and held for resale. This includes items the business has placed on consignment with other parties but excludes items that the business has taken on consignment from other parties. The cost of merchandise includes not only the invoice price less any discounts but also any additional or incidental costs incurred to put the merchandise into place and condition for sale.

Learning Objective 2:

Calculate the cost of an inventory based on (a) specific invoice prices, (b) weighted-average cost, (c) FIFO, and (d) LIFO, and explain the financial statement effects of choosing one method over the others.

Summary

When specific invoice prices are used to price an inventory, each item in the inventory is identified and the cost of the item is determined by referring to the item's purchase invoice. With weighted-average cost, the total cost of the beginning inventory and of purchases is divided by the total number of units available to determine the weighted-average cost per unit. Multiplying this cost by the number of units in the ending inventory yields the cost of the inventory. FIFO prices the ending inventory based on the assumption that the first units purchased are the first units sold. LIFO is based on the assumption that the last units purchased are the first units sold. All of these methods are acceptable.

Learning Objective 3:

Explain the effect of an inventory error on the income statements of the current and succeeding years.

Summary

When the periodic inventory system is used, an error in counting the ending inventory affects assets (inventory), net income (cost of goods sold), and owner's equity. Since the ending inventory is the beginning inventory of the next period, an error at the end of one period affects the cost of goods sold and the net income of the next period. These next period effects offset the financial statement effects in the previous period.

Learning Objective 4:

Describe perpetual inventory systems and prepare entries to record merchandise transactions and maintain subsidiary inventory records under a perpetual inventory system.

Summary

Under a perpetual inventory system, purchases and purchases returns are recorded in the Merchandise Inventory account. At the time sales are recorded, the cost of goods sold is credited to Merchandise Inventory. As a result, the Merchandise Inventory is kept up to date throughout the accounting period.

Learning Objective 5:

Calculate the lower-of-cost-or-market amount of an inventory.

Summary

When lower of cost or market is applied to merchandise inventory, market usually means replacement cost. Lower of cost or market may be applied separately to each product, to major categories of products, or to the merchandise inventory as a whole.

Learning Objective 6:

Use the retail method and the gross profit method to estimate an inventory and calculate merchandise turnover and days' stock on hand.

Summary

When the retail method is used, sales are subtracted from the retail amount of goods available for sale to determine the ending inventory at retail. This is multiplied by the cost ratio to reduce the inventory amount to cost. To calculate the cost ratio, divide the cost of goods available by the retail value of goods available (including markups but excluding markdowns).

With the gross profit method, multiply sales by (1 - the gross profit rate) to estimate cost of goods sold. Then, subtract the answer from the cost of goods available for sale to estimate the cost of the ending inventory.

Analysts use merchandise turnover and days' stock on hand in evaluating a company's short-term liquidity. They also use merchandise turnover to evaluate whether the amount of merchandise kept in inventory is too high or too low.

Learning Objective 7:

Define or explain the words and phrases listed in the chapter glossary.

Summary

See Problem III.

Topical Outline

I. Inventory accounting

   A. Merchandise inventory

      1. The tangible property a merchandising business holds for sale.

      2. Usually the largest current asset of a merchandising concern.

   B. Major objective in inventory accounting

      1. The proper determination of income through the process of matching appropriate costs against revenues.

      2. Means assigning costs of inventory for sale during the accounting period either to cost of goods sold or to ending inventory.

II. Periodic inventory system

   A. Items included on an inventory

      1. All goods owned by the business and held for sale regardless of the physical location of the goods.

      2. All costs incurred in bringing an article to its existing condition and location.

   B. Cost of ending inventory is determined by:

      1. Determining quantity of each item on hand.

      2. Assigning a cost to the quantities on hand.

   C. Cost of goods sold is calculated by subtracting cost of ending inventory from goods available for sale.

   D. Four ways to assign costs

      1. Specific invoice prices

         a. Each inventory item is matched with its invoice price.

         b. This method is of practical use only with relatively high-priced items of which only a few are sold.

      2. Weighted-average cost

         a. Total cost of beginning inventory and purchases is divided by number of units to find average cost per unit.

         b. This method tends to smooth out price fluctuations.

      3. First-in, first-out (FIFO)

         a. Costs are assigned under the assumption that the items in beginning inventory are sold first. (This pricing method may be assumed even if physical flow of goods does not follow this pattern.)

         b. With FIFO method, inventory on the balance sheet most closely approximates current replacement cost.

      4. Last-in, first-out (LIFO)

         a. Costs are assigned under the assumption that the most recent purchases are sold first.

         b. Use of LIFO method results in better matching of current costs and revenues.

         c. LIFO offers a tax advantage to users during a period of rising prices.

III. Accounting principles

A. Principle of consistency—requires a persistent application of an accounting method, period after period.

B. Full-disclosure principle—requires a full disclosure of the nature of any change in accounting methods.

C. Principle of conservatism—when two estimates of amounts to be received or paid in the future are about equally likely, the less optimistic estimate should be used. Inventory cannot be written up to market when market exceeds cost.

D. Principle of materiality—in pricing an inventory, incidental costs of acquiring merchandise may be treated as expenses of the period in which incurred.

IV. Inventory errors in a periodic inventory system

A. An error in determining the end-of-period inventory will cause misstatements in cost of goods sold, gross profit, net income, current assets, and owners' equity.

B. Error will carry forward in succeeding period's cost of goods sold, gross profit, and net income.

C. Errors in cost of goods sold and net income will be offset by errors in the following period.

V. Perpetual inventory system

A. Updates the Merchandise Inventory account after each purchase and each sale.

B. Does not use a Purchases account; cost of items purchased is debited directly to Merchandise Inventory.

C. Requires two entries to record a sale of merchandise.

D. Merchandise Inventory account serves as a controlling account to a subsidiary Merchandise Inventory Ledger, which contains a separate record for each product in stock.

VI. Lower of cost or market

A. Inventory is normally reported on the balance sheet at market value whenever market is lower than cost.

1. Market normally means replacement cost.

2. Merchandise is written down to market because the value of the merchandise to the company has declined.

B. Lower of cost or market pricing is applied either:

1. To the inventory as a whole, or

2. To major categories of products, or

3. Separately to each product in the inventory.

VII. Estimated inventories

A. Retail inventory method

1. Used to estimate ending inventory on the ratios of cost of goods for sale at cost and cost of goods for sale at retail.

2. Satisfactory for interim statements, but a physical inventory should be taken at least once a year.

B. Gross profit method

    1. Similar to retail method, but does not require information about retail price of beginning inventory, purchases, and markups.

    2. Company must know its normal gross profit margin or rate.

VIII. Merchandise turnover

    A. The number of times a company's average inventory was sold during an accounting period.

    B. Calculated as: $\dfrac{\text{Cost of goods sold}}{\text{Average merchandise inventory}}$

IX. Days' stock on hand

    A. An estimate of how many days it will take to convert the inventory on hand at the end of the period into accounts receivable or cash.

    B. Calculated as: $\dfrac{\text{Ending inventory}}{\text{Cost of goods sold}} \times 365$

Problem I

The following statements are either true or false. Place a (T) in the parentheses before each true statement and an (F) before each false statement.

1. ( ) The merchandise inventory of a business includes goods sold FOB destination if they are not yet delivered.

2. ( ) When a perpetual inventory system is used, the dollar amount of ending inventory is determined by counting the units of product on hand, multiplying the count for each product by its cost, and adding the costs for all products.

3. ( ) If prices of goods purchased remain unchanged, then all four methods of assigning costs to goods in the ending inventory would yield the same cost figures.

4. ( ) When first-in, first-out inventory pricing is used, the costs of the first items purchased are assigned to the ending inventory, and the remaining costs are assigned to goods sold.

5. ( ) If prices are rising, then using the LIFO method of pricing inventory will result in the highest net income.

6. ( ) The conservatism principle supports the lower of cost or market rule.

7. ( ) Under the periodic inventory system, an error in ending inventory will carry forward and cause misstatements in the succeeding period's cost of goods sold, gross profit, and net income.

8. ( ) The perpetual inventory system uses a Purchases account to record items purchased.

9. ( ) Using FIFO, the perpetual and periodic inventory systems do not result in the same amounts of sales, cost of goods sold, and end-of-period merchandise inventory.

10. ( ) Lower of cost or market may be applied separately to each product, to major categories of products, or to the merchandise inventory as a whole.

Problem II

You are given several words, phrases, or numbers to choose from in completing each of the following statements or in answering the following questions. In each case select the one that best completes the statement or answers the question and place its letter in the answer space provided.

_____ 1. Cisco Company's ending inventory consists of the following:

Product	Units on Hand	Unit Cost	Replacement Cost per Unit
X	100	$10	$ 8
Y	90	15	14
Z	75	8	10

Replacement cost is determined to be the best measure of market. Lower of cost or market for the inventory applied separately to each product is:

a. $2,950.
b. $2,810.
c. $2,660.
d. $3,100.
e. Cannot be determined from the information given.

_____ 2. Magnum Company began a year and purchased merchandise as follows:

Jan.	1	Beginning inventory	40 units @ $17.00
Feb.	4	Purchased	80 units @ $16.00
May	12	Purchased	80 units @ $16.50
Aug.	9	Purchased	60 units @ $17.50
Nov.	23	Purchased	100 units @ $18.00

The company uses a periodic inventory system and the ending inventory consists of 60 units, 20 from each of the last three purchases. Determine ending inventory assuming costs are assigned on the basis of FIFO.

a. $1,040.
b. $1,000.
c. $1,069.
d. $1,080.
e. $1,022.

_____ 3. Linder Company began a year and purchased merchandise as follows:

Jan.	1	Beginning inventory	40 units @ $17.00
Feb.	4	Purchased	80 units @ $16.00
May	12	Purchased	80 units @ $16.50
Aug.	9	Purchased	60 units @ $17.50
Nov.	23	Purchased	100 units @ $18.00

The company uses a periodic inventory system and the ending inventory consists of 60 units, 20 from each of the last three purchases. Determine ending inventory assuming costs are assigned on the basis of LIFO.

a. $1,040.
b. $1,000.
c. $1,022.
d. $ 980.
e. $1,080.

_____ 4. Box Company began a year and purchased merchandise as follows:

Jan.	1	Beginning inventory	40 units @ $17.00
Feb.	4	Purchased	80 units @ $16.00
May	12	Purchased	80 units @ $16.50
Aug.	9	Purchased	60 units @ $17.50
Nov.	23	Purchased	100 units @ $18.00

The company uses a periodic inventory system and the ending inventory consists of 60 units, 20 from each of the last three purchases. Determine ending inventory assuming costs are assigned on the basis of specific invoice prices.

a. $1,000.
b. $1,022.
c. $1,040.
d. $1,080.
e. $ 990.

5. Crow Company began a year and purchased merchandise as follows:

Jan. 1	Beginning inventory	....	40 units @ $17.00
Feb. 4	Purchased	....	80 units @ $16.00
May 12	Purchased	....	80 units @ $16.50
Aug. 9	Purchased	....	60 units @ $17.50
Nov. 23	Purchased	....	100 units @ $18.00

The company uses a periodic inventory system and the ending inventory consists of 60 units, 20 from each of the last three purchases. Determine ending inventory assuming costs are assigned on a weighted-average basis.

a. $1,022.00
b. $1,040.00
c. $1,080.00
d. $1,000.00
e. $1,042.50

6. Atlantis Company uses a periodic inventory system and made an error at the end of year 1 that caused its year 1 ending inventory to be understated by $5,000. What effect does this error have on the company's financial statements?

a. Net income is understated; assets are understated.
b. Net income is understated; assets are overstated.
c. Net income is overstated; assets are understated.
d. Net income is overstated; assets are overstated.
e. Net income is overstated; assets are correctly stated.

7. Sanders Company wants to prepare interim financial statements for the first quarter of 19X1. The company uses a periodic inventory system and has an average gross profit rate of 30%. Based on the following information, use the gross profit method to prepare an estimate of the March 31 inventory.

January 1, beginning inventory	$ 97,000
Purchases	214,000
Purchases returns	2,000
Transportation-in	4,000
Sales	404,000
Sales returns	5,000

a. $ 33,700.
b. $193,300.
c. $119,700.
d. $179,900.
e. $ 26,700.

8. Trador Company's ending inventory at December 31, 19X2 and 19X1, was $210,000 and $146,000, respectively. Cost of goods sold for 19X2 was $832,000 and $780,000 for 19X1. Calculate Trador's merchandise turnover for 19X2.

a. 4.7 times.
b. 4.5 times.
c. 4.0 times.
d. 3.8 times.
e. Cannot be determined from the information given.

_____ 9. Refer to the information presented in question 8. Calculate Trador's days' stock on hand for 19X2.

    a. 78.1 days.
    b. 80.6 days.
    c. 66.1 days.
    d. 92.1 days.
    e. 68.3 days.

Problem III

Many of the important ideas and concepts discussed in Chapter 9 are reflected in the following list of key terms. Test your understanding of these terms by matching the appropriate definitions with the terms. Record the number identifying the most appropriate definition in the blank space next to each term.

_____ Conservatism principle

_____ Consignee

_____ Consignor

_____ Consistency principle

_____ Days' stock on hand

_____ First-in, first-out inventory pricing (FIFO)

_____ Gross profit inventory method

_____ Interim statements

_____ Inventory ticket

_____ Last-in, first-out inventory pricing (LIFO)

_____ Lower of cost or market (LCM)

_____ Merchandise turnover

_____ Net realizable value

_____ Retail inventory method

_____ Retail method cost ratio

_____ Specific invoice inventory pricing

_____ Weighted-average inventory pricing

1. The required method of reporting merchandise inventory on the balance sheet, in which market is normally defined as replacement cost on the date of the balance sheet.

2. The pricing of an inventory under the assumption that the first items received were the first items sold.

3. An inventory pricing system in which the unit prices of the beginning inventory and of each purchase are weighted by the number of units in the beginning inventory and each purchase. The total of these amounts is then divided by the total number of units available for sale to find the unit cost of the ending inventory and of the units that were sold.

4. The number of times a company's average inventory was sold during an accounting period, calculated by dividing cost of goods sold by the average merchandise inventory balance.

5. The accounting requirement that a company use the same accounting methods period after period so that the financial statements of succeeding periods will be comparable.

6. An estimate of how many days it will take to convert the inventory on hand at the end of the period into accounts receivable or cash; calculated by dividing the ending inventory by cost of goods sold and multiplying the result by 365.

7. The ratio of goods available for sale at cost to goods available for sale at retail prices.

8. An owner of goods who ships them to another party who will then sell the goods for the owner.

9. A procedure for estimating an ending inventory in which the past gross profit rate is used to estimate cost of goods sold, which is then subtracted from the cost of goods available for sale to determine the estimated ending inventory.

10. The pricing of an inventory where the purchase invoice of each item in the ending inventory is identified and used to determine the cost assigned to the inventory.

11. A form attached to the counted items in the process of taking a physical inventory.

12. The pricing of an inventory under the assumption that the last items received were the first items sold.

13. The accounting principle that guides accountants to select the less optimistic estimate when two estimates of amounts to be received or paid are about equally likely.

14. Monthly or quarterly financial statements prepared in between the regular year-end statements.

15. A method for estimating an ending inventory based on the ratio of the amount of goods for sale at cost to the amount of goods for sale at marked selling prices.

16. One who receives and holds goods owned by another party for the purpose of selling the goods for the owner.

17. The expected sales price of an item less any additional costs to sell.

Problem IV

Complete the following by filling in the blanks.

1. Consistency in the use of an inventory costing method is particularly important if there is to be

_____ .

2. If a running record is maintained for each inventory item of the number of units received as units are received, the number of units sold as units are sold, and the number of units remaining after each

receipt or sale, the inventory system is called _____ .

3. When a company changes its accounting procedures, the _____ principle requires that the nature of the change, justification for the change, and the effect of the change

on _____ be disclosed in the notes accompanying the financial statements.

4. With a periodic inventory system, an error in taking an end-of-period inventory will cause a misstatement

of periodic net income for _____ (one, two) accounting periods because

_____

_____

_____ .

5. When identical items are purchased during an accounting period at different costs, a problem arises as to which costs apply to the ending inventory and which apply to the goods sold. There are at least four commonly used ways of assigning costs to inventory and to goods sold. They are:

   a. _____ ;

   b. _____ ;

   c. _____ ;

   d. _____ .

6. A major objective of accounting for inventories is the proper determination of periodic net income

   through the process of matching _____ and _____ .
   The matching process consists of determining how much of the cost of the goods that were for sale

   during an accounting period should be deducted from the period's _____ and

   how much should be carried forward as _____ , to be
   matched against a future period's revenues.

7. Although changing back and forth from one inventory costing method to another might allow management to report the incomes it would prefer, the accounting principle of _____ requires a company to use the same pricing method period after period unless it can justify the change.

8. In the gross profit method of estimating an ending inventory, an average _____ _____ rate is used to determine estimated cost of goods sold, and the ending inventory is then estimated by subtracting estimated _____ from the cost of goods available for sale.

9. In separating cost of goods available for sale into cost of goods sold and cost of goods unsold, the procedures for assigning a cost to the ending inventory are also the means of determining _____ _____ because whatever portion of the cost of goods available for sale is assigned to ending inventory, the remainder goes to _____ .

10. Cost of an inventory item includes _____ _____ _____ _____ _____ .

11. Use of the lower-of-cost-or-market rule places an inventory on the balance sheet at a _____ figure. The argument in favor of this rule provides that any loss should be _____ in the year the loss occurs.

12. When recording a sale of merchandise using a _____ (perpetual, periodic) inventory system, two journal entries must be made. One entry records the revenue received for the sale and the second entry debits the _____ account.

Problem V

A company uses a perpetual inventory system and during a year had the following beginning inventory, purchases, and sales of Product Z:

Jan. 1	Inventory	200 units @ $0.50 = $100
Mar. 15	Purchased	400 units @ 0.50 = 200
Apr. 1	Sold	300 units
June 3	Purchased	300 units @ 0.60 = 180
July 1	Sold	200 units
Oct. 8	Purchased	600 units @ 0.70 = 420
Nov. 1	Sold	500 units
Dec. 15	Purchased	500 units @ 0.80 = 400

In the spaces below show the cost that should be assigned to the ending inventory and to the goods sold under the following assumptions:

	Portions Assigned to—	
	Ending Inventory	Cost of Goods Sold
1. A first-in, first-out basis was used to price the ending inventory	$	$
2. A last-in, first-out basis was used to price the ending inventory	$	$

Problem VI

The following end-of-period information about a store's beginning inventory, purchases, and sales is available.

	At Cost	At Retail
Beginning inventory	$ 9,600	$13,000
Net purchases	54,400	69,100
Transportation-in	1,680	
Net sales		69,000

The above information is to be used to estimate the store's ending inventory by the retail method.

1. The store had goods available for sale during the year calculated as follows:

	At Cost	At Retail
Beginning inventory	$_____	$_____
Net purchases	_____	_____
Transportation-in	_____	_____
Goods available for sale	$_____	$_____

2. The store's cost ratio was:

   $_____ / $_____ × 100 = _____

3. Of the goods the store had available for sale at market retail prices during the year, the following is gone because of --

   Net sales at retail .... _____

   Which left the store an estimated ending inventory at retail $_____

4. And when the store's cost ratio is applied to this estimated ending inventory at retail, the estimated ending inventory at cost is .... $_____

The store took a physical inventory and counted only $12,850 of merchandise on hand (at retail). Calculate the inventory shortage at cost.

Solutions for Chapter 9

Problem I

1.	T	6.	T
2.	F	7.	T
3.	T	8.	F
4.	F	9.	F
5.	F	10.	T

Problem II

1.	C	6.	A
2.	D	7.	A
3.	B	8.	A
4.	C	9.	D
5.	A		

Problem III

Conservatism principle	13
Consignee	16
Consignor	8
Consistency principle	5
Days' stock on hand	6
FIFO inventory pricing	2
Gross profit inventory method	9
Interim statements	14
Inventory ticket	11
LIFO inventory pricing	12
Lower of cost or market	1
Merchandise turnover	4
Net realizable value	17
Retail inventory method	15
Retail method cost ratio	7
Specific invoice inventory pricing	10
Weighted-average inventory pricing	3

Problem IV

1. comparability in the financial statements prepared period after period

2. a perpetual inventory system

3. full-disclosure, net income

4. two, the ending inventory of one period becomes the beginning inventory of the next

5. (a) specific invoice prices; (b) weighted-average cost; (c) first-in, first-out; (d) last-in, first-out

6. costs, revenues, revenues, merchandise inventory

7. consistency

8. gross profit, cost of goods sold

9. cost of goods sold, cost of goods sold

10. the invoice price, less the discount, plus any additional incidental costs necessary to put the item in place and in condition for sale

11. conservative, recognized

12. perpetual, cost of goods sold

Problem V

	Portions Assigned to—	
	Ending Inventory	Cost of Goods Sold
1.	$750	$550
2.	550	750

Problem VI

	At Cost	At Retail
Goods for sale:		
Beginning inventory	$ 9,600	$13,000
Net purchases	54,400	69,100
Transportation-in	1,680	
Goods available for sale	$65,680	$82,100
Cost ratio: $65,680/$82,100 × 100 = 80%		
Net sales at retail		69,000
Ending inventory at retail		$13,100
Ending inventory at cost ($13,100 × 80%)	$10,480	

Inventory shortage at cost:
    $13,100 − $12,850 = $250
    $250 × 80% = $200

10 Plant and Equipment

Learning Objective 1:

Describe the differences between plant assets and other kinds of assets, and calculate the cost and record the purchase of plant assets.

Summary

Plant assets are tangible items that have a useful life longer than one accounting period. Plant assets are not held for sale but are used in the production or sale of other assets or services. The cost of plant assets includes all normal and reasonable expenditures necessary to get the assets in place and ready to use. The cost of a lump-sum purchase should be allocated among the individual assets based on their relative market values.

Learning Objective 2:

Explain depreciation accounting (including the reasons for depreciation), calculate depreciation by the straight-line and units-of-production methods, and calculate depreciation after revising the estimated useful life of an asset.

Summary

The cost of plant assets that have limited service lives must be allocated to the accounting periods that benefit from their use. The straight-line method of depreciation divides the cost minus salvage value by the number of periods in the service life of the asset to determine the depreciation expense of each period. The units-of-production method divides the cost minus salvage value by the estimated number of units the asset will produce to determine the depreciation per unit. If the estimated useful life of a plant asset is changed, the remaining cost to be depreciated is spread over the remaining (revised) useful life of the asset.

Learning Objective 3:

Describe the use of accelerated depreciation for financial accounting and tax accounting purposes and calculate accelerated depreciation under *(a)* the declining-balance method, and *(b)* the Modified Accelerated Cost Recovery System.

Summary

Accelerated depreciation methods such as the declining-balance method are acceptable for financial accounting purposes if they are based on realistic estimates of useful life. However, they are not widely used at the present time. The Modified Accelerated Cost Recovery System (MACRS), which is used for tax purposes, is not based on realistic estimates of useful life. Thus, MACRS is not acceptable for financial accounting purposes.

Learning Objective 4:

Describe the difference between revenue and capital expenditures and account properly for costs such as repairs and betterments incurred after the original purchase of plant assets.

Summary

The benefit of revenue expenditures expires during the current period. Thus, revenue expenditures are debited to expense accounts and matched with current revenues. Capital expenditures are debited to asset accounts because they benefit future periods. Ordinary repairs are revenue expenditures. Examples of capital expenditures include extraordinary repairs and betterments. Amounts paid for assets with low costs are technically capital expenditures but can be treated as revenue expenditures if they are not material.

Learning Objective 5:

Prepare entries to account for the disposal or exchange of plant assets and explain the use of total asset turnover in evaluating a company's efficiency in using its assets.

Summary

When a plant asset is discarded or sold, the cost and accumulated depreciation are removed from the accounts. Any cash proceeds are recorded and compared to the asset's book value to determine gain or loss. When nonmonetary assets are exchanged and they are dissimilar, the new asset is recorded at its fair value, and either a gain or a loss on disposal is recognized. When similar assets are exchanged, losses are recognized but gains are not. Instead, the new asset account is debited for the book value of the old asset plus any cash paid. Total asset turnover measures the efficiency of a company's use of its assets to generate sales.

Learning Objective 6:

Define or explain the words and phrases listed in the chapter glossary.

Summary

See Problem III.

Topical Outline

I. Plant assets

    A. Tangible assets that are used in the production or sale of other assets or services and that have an expected service life longer than one accounting period.

    B. Cost of a plant asset

        1. Includes all normal and reasonable expenditures necessary to get the asset in place and ready to use. This includes items such as invoice price and sales tax, less early payment discount, plus any freight, assembly, and installation costs.

        2. When constructed for own use, includes such costs as material, labor, indirect overhead, design fees, building permits, and insurance during construction.

        3. When land is purchased as a building site, includes purchase price, commissions, title insurance, legal fees, accrued property taxes, surveying, clearing, landscaping, and local government assessments (current or future) for streets, sewers, etc. Land should also include the price of any old buildings that must be removed and removal costs (less salvage value) of the old buildings.

        4. Must be allocated on a fair basis, such as relative appraisal values, if two or more assets are purchased for one price.

    C. Service life (or useful life)—the length of time a plant asset will be used in the operations of the business. Factors in addition to wear and tear which can determine the service life of an asset include:

        1. Inadequacy—a condition in which the capacity of plant assets becomes too small for the productive demands of the business.

        2. Obsolescence—a condition in which, because of new inventions and improvements, a plant asset can no longer be used to produce goods or services with a competitive advantage.

    D. Salvage value—the amount that management expects to receive at the end of a plant asset's service life through a sale or as a trade-in allowance on the purchase of a new asset.

II. Depreciation—the expiration of the usefulness of plant and equipment

    A. The process of allocating and charging the cost (minus estimated salvage value) of a plant asset to the accounting periods that benefit from its use.

    B. Typical methods of allocating depreciation

        1. Straight-line—a method that allocates an equal portion of the total depreciation for a plant asset (cost minus salvage) to each accounting period in its service life. This is the method used by most companies.

        2. Units-of-production—a method that allocates an equal portion of the total depreciation for a plant asset (cost minus salvage) to each unit of product or service that it produces, or on a similar basis, such as hours of use or miles driven.

    C. For assets acquired or disposed of at some time other than the beginning or end of a year, only a partial year's depreciation should be recorded.

    D. Depreciation in the financial statements

        1. The cost of plant assets and their accumulated depreciation must be shown on the balance sheet or in related footnotes.

        2. To satisfy the full-disclosure principle, the depreciation method or methods used must be disclosed in a balance sheet footnote or other manner.

3. Since depreciation is a process of allocating cost, the cost (net of depreciation) is not intended to represent market value.

4. Accumulated depreciation on the balance sheet does not represent funds accumulated to buy new assets when the presently owned assets must be replaced.

E. Revising depreciation rates

1. If new information shows that the original prediction of useful life was inaccurate, the estimate of annual depreciation expense should be revised by spreading the remaining cost to be depreciated over the revised remaining useful life.

2. A revision of the predicted useful life or salvage value of a plant asset is a change in an accounting estimate and should be reflected only in future financial statements.

III. Accelerated depreciation

A. Produces larger depreciation charges during the early years of an asset's life and smaller charges in the later years.

B. Declining-balance depreciation

1. A depreciation rate of up to twice the straight-line rate is applied each year to the asset's beginning book value. Salvage value is not used in the calculation.

2. When the depreciation rate used is twice the straight-line rate, the method is called double-declining-balance depreciation.

C. Accelerated depreciation for tax purposes

1. Federal income tax law requires the Modified Accelerated Cost Recovery System (MACRS) for assets purchased after 1986. Assets are classified into 3-year, 5-year, 7-year, 10-year, 15-year, 20-year, 27 1/2-year, and 31 1/2-year classes. Either straight-line or an accelerated method may be used with these class lives.

2. When calculating depreciation for tax purposes under MACRS, salvage values are ignored, and the half-year convention (which assumes assets are acquired and retired at mid-year) must be used.

3. MACRS is not consistent with generally accepted accounting principles, and is therefore not acceptable for financial accounting purposes, because it allocates depreciation over an arbitrary period that is usually much shorter than the estimated service life of an asset.

IV. Revenue and capital expenditures—made to operate, maintain, repair, or improve plant assets after their initial purchase

A. A revenue expenditure should appear on the current income statement as an expense and be deducted from the period's revenues because it does not provide a material benefit in future periods.

1. Ordinary repairs—made to keep an asset in normal, good operating condition.

2. Plant assets with low costs—according to the materiality principle, may be charged directly to an expense account at the time of purchase.

B. A capital (or balance sheet) expenditure produces economic benefits that do not fully expire before the end of the current period. Because a capital expenditure increases or improves the kind or amount of service an asset provides, it is debited to an asset account and reported on the balance sheet. These types of expenditures usually result in a recalculation of annual depreciation expense for the remaining useful life of the asset.

1. Extraordinary repairs—major repairs that extend an asset's service life beyond the original estimate. They are usually debited to the asset's accumulated depreciation account.

2. Betterments—modifications or additions to an asset that make it more productive or efficient, but do not necessarily extend its useful life. They are typically debited to the asset account.

V. Plant asset disposals and exchanges

   A. Assets may be retired, sold, or exchanged due to wear and tear, obsolescence, inadequacy, or damage by fire or other accident.

   B. Journal entries related to a disposal should:

      1. Bring depreciation expense and accumulated depreciation up to the date of the disposal.

      2. Remove asset and accumulated depreciation account balances relating to the disposal.

      3. Record any cash received or paid as a result of the disposal.

      4. Record any gain or loss that results from comparing the book value of the asset with the cash received or paid as a result of the disposal.

   C. Exchanges of dissimilar assets

      1. Compare the book value of the asset given up with the fair value of the assets received and record any gain or loss on the exchange.

      2. Record the new asset at its fair market value.

   D. Exchanges of similar assets (when the exchange includes a cash payment or when no cash is received or paid)

      1. When the trade-in allowance is less than the book value of the old asset:

         a. Recognize a loss.

         b. Record the new asset at its fair makret value.

      2. When the trade-in allowance is more than the book value of the old asset:

         a. Do not recognize a gain.

         b. Record the new asset at the old asset's book value plus cash paid.

VI. Total asset turnover

   A. A measure of how efficiently a company uses its assets to generate sales.

   B. Calculated by dividing net sales by average total assets.

Problem I

The following statements are either true or false. Place a (T) in the parentheses before each true statement and an (F) before each false statement.

1. ( ) Cost is the basis for recording the acquisition of a plant asset.

2. ( ) The cost of a plant asset constructed by a business for its own use would include depreciation on the machinery used in constructing the asset.

3. ( ) Depreciation is a process of determining the value of assets.

4. ( ) The cost of extraordinary repairs which extend the service life of an asset should be debited to a Repairs Expense account.

5. ( ) The service life of a plant asset can be affected by inadequacy or obsolescence.

6. ( ) Accelerated depreciation methods increase taxable income in the early years of an asset's life.

7. ( ) Straight-line depreciation charges each year of an asset's life with an equal amount of expense.

8. ( ) Double-declining-balance depreciation applies twice the straight-line rate to the beginning book value of an asset to calculate each year's depreciation expense.

9. ( ) When similar assets are exchanged, losses are recognized but gains are not.

10. ( ) Total asset turnover is calculated by dividing average total assets by net sales.

11. ( ) The cost of making an ordinary repair to a machine should be classified as a revenue expenditure.

12. ( ) The debit balance in accumulated depreciation represents funds accumulated to buy new assets when the presently owned assets must be replaced.

13. ( ) If a cost is incurred to modify an existing plant asset for the purpose of making it more efficient or more productive, the cost should be classified as an extraordinary repair.

14. ( ) A betterment is recorded by reducing accumulated depreciation.

15. ( ) For assets purchased after 1986, the tax law provides a system of accelerated depreciation called the Modified Accelerated Cost Recovery System.

Problem II

You are given several words, phrases, or numbers to choose from in completing each of the following statements or in answering the following questions. In each case select the one that best completes the statement or answers the question and place its letter in the answer space provided.

_____ 1. Jocelyn Leland, CPA, paid $165,000 to purchase approximately two acres of land and the building on it to be used as an office. The building was appraised at $84,000 and the land was appraised at $126,000. What amount should be debited to the Land account?

a. $165,000.
b. $211,000.
c. $126,000.
d. $ 66,000.
e. $ 99,000.

_____ 2. Flintstone Company depreciated a machine that cost $21,600 on a straight-line basis for three years under the assumption it would have a five-year life and a $3,600 trade-in value. At that point, the manager realized that the machine had three years of remaining useful life, after which it would have an estimated $2,160 trade-in value. Determine the amount of depreciation to be charged against the machine during each of the remaining years in its life.

   a. $3,240.
   b. $1,800.
   c. $2,640.
   d. $2,880.
   e. $3,888.

_____ 3. Busy Bee Industries installed a machine in its factory at a cost of $84,000 on May 1, 19X3. The machine's useful life is estimated at eight years with a $9,000 salvage value. Determine the machine's 19X3 depreciation using the double-declining-balance method of depreciation.

   a. $14,000.
   b. $10,500.
   c. $21,000.
   d. $12,500.
   e. $18,750.

_____ 4. Spacely's Sprockets purchased a machine on September 1 for $400,000. The machine's useful life was estimated at six years or 500,000 units of product with a $25,000 trade-in value. During its second year, the machine produced 87,000 units of product. Assuming units-of-production depreciation, calculate the machine's second-year depreciation.

   a. $69,600.
   b. $66,667.
   c. $65,250.
   d. $62,500.
   e. $31,250.

_____ 5. A machine that cost $40,000 and had been depreciated $30,000 was traded in on a new machine of like purpose having an estimated 10-year life and priced at $50,000. If a $13,000 trade-in allowance was received on the old machine, at what amount should the new machine be recorded in the accounts?

   a. $37,000.
   b. $40,000.
   c. $47,000.
   d. $50,000.
   e. $53,000.

_____ 6. On January 1, 19X1, a machine with a salvage value of $12,000 and an estimated service life of five years was purchased for $72,000. For tax purposes, the machine is in the three-year class and the half-year convention is required. Calculate depreciation expense for 19X1 assuming straight-line depreciation under MACRS.

   a. $10,000.
   b. $12,000.
   c. $14,400.
   d. $20,000.
   e. $24,000.

_____ 7. The Romeo Company exchanged its used bottle-capping machine for a new bottle-capping machine. The old machine cost $14,000, and the new one had a cash price of $19,000. Romeo had taken $12,000 depreciation on the old machine and was allowed a $500 trade-in allowance. What gain or loss should be recorded on the exchange?

    a. No gain or loss.
    b. $ 500 gain.
    c. $1,500 loss.
    d. $1,500 gain.
    e. $4,500 gain.

_____ 8. Cherokee Company had a bulldozer destroyed by fire. The bulldozer originally cost $16,000, but insurance paid only $14,200. Accumulated depreciation on this bulldozer was $2,000. The gain or loss from the fire is:

    a. No gain or loss.
    b. $ 200 gain.
    c. $ 200 loss.
    d. $ 1,800 loss.
    e. $16,000 loss.

_____ 9. Following is selected year-end financial statement information from the Mega Life Company:

	12/31/X2	12/31/X3
Total assets	$18,500	$20,000
Total liabilities	12,750	11,900
Net sales	73,000	88,550
Total expenses ...	48,200	53,150

What is the total asset turnover for 19X3?

    a. 4.4
    b. 2.9
    c. 0.2
    d. 4.6
    e. 1.8

_____ 10. Fleet Lines made a $3,000 modification to one of its trucks that made the truck more efficient. The $3,000 should be debited to which account?

    a. Trucks.
    b. Accumulated Depreciation, Trucks.
    c. Betterments.
    d. Extraordinary Repairs.
    e. Capital Expenditures.

Problem III

Many of the important ideas and concepts discussed in Chapter 10 are reflected in the following list of key terms. Test your understanding of these terms by matching the appropriate definitions with the terms. Record the number identifying the most appropriate definition in the blank space next to each term.

_____ Accelerated depreciation	_____ Modified Accelerated Cost Recovery System (MACRS)	
_____ Balance sheet expenditure	_____ Obsolescence	
_____ Betterment	_____ Ordinary repairs	
_____ Book value	_____ Revenue expenditure	
_____ Capital expenditure	_____ Salvage value	
_____ Change in an accounting estimate	_____ Service life	
_____ Declining-balance depreciation	_____ Straight-line depreciation	
_____ Extraordinary repairs	_____ Total asset turnover	
_____ Inadequacy	_____ Units-of-production depreciation	
_____ Land improvements		

1. The system of depreciation required by federal income tax law for assets placed in service after 1986.

2. The amount that management predicts will be recovered at the end of a plant asset's service life through a sale or as a trade-in allowance on the purchase of a new asset.

3. A condition in which, because of new inventions and improvements, a plant asset can no longer be used to produce goods or services with a competitive advantage.

4. A method that allocates an equal portion of the total depreciation for a plant asset (cost minus salvage) to each unit of product or service that it produces, or on a similar basis, such as hours of use or miles driven.

5. Assets that increase the usefulness of land but that have a limited useful life and are subject to depreciation.

6. A measure of how efficiently a company uses its assets to generate sales; calculated by dividing net sales by average total assets.

7. A depreciation method in which a plant asset's depreciation charge for the period is determined by applying a constant depreciation rate (up to twice the straight-line rate) each year to the asset's beginning book value.

8. Another name for capital expenditure.

9. A method that allocates an equal portion of the total depreciation for a plant asset (cost minus salvage) to each accounting period in its service life.

10. The amount assigned to an item in the accounting records and in the financial statements; for a plant asset, it is the original cost less accumulated depreciation.

11. Depreciation methods that produce larger depreciation charges during the early years of an asset's life and smaller charges in the later years.

12. The length of time in which a plant asset will be used in the operations of the business.

13. A condition in which the capacity of plant assets becomes too small for the productive demands of the business.

14. A modification to an asset to make it more efficient, usually by replacing one of its components with an improved or superior component.

15. An expenditure that produces economic benefits that do not fully expire before the end of the current period; because it creates or adds to existing assets, it should appear on the balance sheet as the cost of an asset.

16. A change in a calculated amount used in the financial statements that results from new information or subsequent developments and from better insight or improved judgment.

17. An expenditure that should appear on the current income statement as an expense and be deducted from the period's revenues because it does not provide a material benefit in future periods.

18. Repairs made to keep a plant asset in normal, good operating condition; treated as a revenue expenditure.

19. Major repairs that extend the service life of a plant asset beyond original expectations; treated as a capital expenditure.

Problem IV

Complete the following by filling in the blanks.

1. Land has an unlimited useful life, is not consumed when it is used, and therefore is not subject to
   _____. Costs that increase the usefulness of the land, such as parking lots or fences, should be classified as _____.

2. There are several factors that affect the useful life of some assets. These factors include:
   a) _____
   b) _____
   c) _____

3. The method of depreciation currently used by most companies for financial accounting purposes is
   _____

   The most commonly used accelerated method of depreciation for financial accounting purposes is
   _____

4. While MACRS is required for tax purposes, it is not acceptable for financial accounting because it allocates depreciation over an arbitrary recovery period that is _____.
   _____

5. Two types of revenue expenditures are: (1) _____ repairs and (2) purchases of
   _____. Two types of capital expenditures are: (1)
   _____ repairs and (2) _____.

6. The tax advantage of accelerated depreciation is that _____
   _____.

7. Trucks held for sale by a dealer and land held for future expansion are not classified as plant assets because _____.

8. Depreciation allocates and charges the cost of an asset's usefulness to _____
   _____.

   Depreciation does not measure the asset's decline in _____ nor its physical
   _____.

Fundamental Accounting Principles, 14th Edition

9. The book value of a plant asset is its "value" as shown by the books and consists of its

_____ minus its _____.

10. Regardless of what leads to a disposal of a plant asset, the journal entry or entries related to the disposal should:

(a) Record _____ and _____
up to the date of the disposal.

(b) Remove the _____ and _____
account balances relating to the disposal.

(c) Record any _____ as a result of the disposal.

(d) Record any _____ or _____ that results from comparing

the _____ of the asset with any cash received or paid as a result of the disposal.

Problem V

A machine was purchased for $7,000, terms 2/10, n/60, FOB vendor's factory. The invoice was paid within the discount period along with $175 of freight charges. The machine was installed on a special concrete base by the employees of the company that bought it. The concrete base and special power connections for the machine cost $575, and the wages of the employees during the period in which they installed the machine amounted to $425. The employees accidentally dropped the machine while moving it onto its special base, causing damages to the machine which cost $125 to repair. As a result of all this, the cost of the machine for accounting purposes should be:

$_____

Problem VI

A machine with a cost of $8,000, an estimated eight-year service life, and an $800 salvage value, was purchased on July 1, 19X1. It was estimated that the machine would produce 144,000 units of product during its life, and it produced 10,000 units during its first year. The depreciation expense for 19X1 was:

1. $_____ calculated on a straight-line basis.

2. $_____ calculated using the units-of-production method.

3. $_____ calculated using the double-declining-balance method.

Problem VII

A machine that cost $45,000 and had been depreciated $20,000 was traded in on a new machine that had a cash price of $35,000. After taking into account the trade-in allowance, the balance was paid in cash. Present a general journal entry to record the trade under each of the following unrelated assumptions:

(a) The trade-in allowance was $28,000, and the new machine was a similar asset.

(b) The trade-in allowance was $21,000, and the new machine was a similar asset.

(c) The trade-in allowance was $33,000, and the new machine was a dissimilar asset.

Problem VIII

In April of 19X1, a company purchased a heavy, general-purpose truck for $50,000. The truck is expected to last eight years and have a salvage value of $10,000. For tax purposes, the truck is in the five-year class, and the half-year convention is required. The company is considering two depreciation alternatives for tax purposes: (a) straight-line depreciation under MACRS, or (b) accelerated depreciation under MACRS. (The MACRS accelerated depreciation rates provided by the IRS for assets in the five-year class are: Year 1, 20.00%; Year 2, 32.00%; Year 3, 19.20%; Years 4 & 5, 11.52%; Year 6, 5.76%.) Show the amount of depreciation, if any, for each of the years shown below under each of the alternatives.

Year	MACRS Straight-Line Depreciation	MACRS Accelerated Depreciation
19X1	_____	_____
19X2	_____	_____
19X3	_____	_____
19X4	_____	_____
19X5	_____	_____
19X6	_____	_____
19X7	_____	_____
19X8	_____	_____
Totals	_____	_____

Solutions for Chapter 10

Problem I

1.	T	9.	T
2.	T	10.	F
3.	F	11.	T
4.	F	12.	F
5.	T	13.	F
6.	F	14.	F
7.	T	15.	T
8.	T		

Problem II

1.	E	6.	B
2.	D	7.	C
3.	A	8.	B
4.	C	9.	D
5.	C	10.	A

Problem III

Accelerated depreciation	11
Balance sheet expenditure	8 or 15
Betterment	14
Book value	10
Capital expenditure	15
Change in accounting estimate	16
Declining-balance depreciation	7
Extraordinary repairs	19
Inadequacy	13
Land improvements	5
Modified Accelerated Cost Recovery System (MACRS)	1
Obsolescence	3
Ordinary repairs	18
Revenue expenditure	17
Salvage value	2
Service life	12
Straight-line depreciation	9
Total asset turnover	6
Units-of-production depreciation	4

Problem IV

1. depreciation; land improvements

2. (a) wear and tear
   (b) inadequacy
   (c) obsolescence

3. straight-line; declining-balance

4. usually much shorter than the estimated service life of an asset

5. ordinary; assets with low costs; extraordinary; betterments

6. the payment of income taxes is deferred

7. they are not being used in the production or sale of other assets or services

8. the accounting periods that benefit from the asset's use; market value; deterioration

9. cost; accumulated depreciation

10. (a) depreciation expense; accumulated depreciation
    (b) asset; accumulated depreciation
    (c) cash received or paid
    (d) gain; loss; book value

Problem V

$7,000 - ($7,000 \times 2\%) + $175 + $575 + $425 = $8,035$

Problem VI

1. ($8,000 - $800)/8 x 6/12 = $450

2. [($8,000 - $800)/144,000] x 10,000 = $500

3. (100%/8) x 2 = 25% double-declining-balance rate
   $8,000 x 25% x 6/12 = $1,000

Problem VII

(a)	Machinery	32,000.00	
	Accumulated Depreciation, Machinery	20,000.00	
	Cash ($35,000 – $28,000)		7,000.00
	Machinery		45,000.00
(b)	Machinery	35,000.00	
	Accumulated Depreciation, Machinery	20,000.00	
	Loss on Exchange of Machinery	4,000.00	
	Cash ($35,000 – $21,000)		14,000.00
	Machinery		45,000.00
(c)	Machinery	35,000.00	
	Accumulated Depreciation, Machinery	20,000.00	
	Gain on Exchange of Machinery		8,000.00
	Cash ($35,000 – $33,000)		2,000.00
	Machinery		45,000.00

Problem VIII

Year	MACRS Straight-Line Depreciation	MACRS Accelerated Depreciation
19X1	$ 5,000	$10,000
19X2	10,000	16,000
19X3	10,000	9,600
19X4	10,000	5,760
19X5	10,000	5,760
19X6	5,000	2,880
19X7	0	0
19X8	0	0
Totals	$50,000	$50,000

11 Natural Resources, Intangible Assets, and Long-Term Investments

Learning Objective 1:

Identify assets that should be classified as natural resources or as intangible assets and prepare entries to account for them, including entries to record depletion and amortization.

Summary

The cost of a natural resource is recorded in an asset account. Then, depletion of the natural resource is recorded by allocating the cost to expense according to a units-of-production basis. The depletion is credited to an accumulated depletion account. Intangible assets are recorded at the cost incurred to purchase the assets. The allocation of intangible asset cost to expense is done on a straight-line basis and is called amortization. Normally, amortization is recorded with credits made directly to the asset account instead of a contra account.

Learning Objective 2:

State the criteria for classifying assets as long-term investments and describe the categories of securities that are classified as long-term investments.

Summary

Securities investments are classified as current assets if they are held as a source of cash to be used in current operations and if they mature within one year or the current operating cycle of the business or are marketable. All other investments in securities are long-term investments, which also include assets held for a special purpose and not used in operations.

Long-term investments in securities are classified in four groups: (a) debt securities held to maturity, (b) debt and equity securities available for sale, (c) equity securities when the investor has a significant influence over the investee, and (d) equity securities when the investor controls the investee.

Learning Objective 3:

Describe the methods used to report long-term securities investments in the financial statements.

Summary

Debt held to maturity is reported at its original cost adjusted for amortization of any difference between cost and maturity value. Debt and equity securities available for sale are reported at their fair values with unrealized gains or losses shown in the stockholders' equity section of the balance sheet. Gains and losses realized on the sale of the investments are reported in the income statement.

The equity method is used if the investor has a significant influence over the investee. This situation usually exists when the investor owns 20% or more of the investee's voting stock. If an investor owns more than 50% of another corporation's voting stock and controls the investee, the investor's financial reports are prepared on a consolidated basis.

Under the equity method, the investor records its share of the investee's earnings with a debit to the investment account and a credit to a revenue account. Dividends received satisfy the investor's equity claims, and reduce the investment account balance.

Learning Objective 4:

Describe the primary accounting problems of having investments in international operations and prepare entries to account for sales to foreign customers.

Summary

If a U.S. company makes a credit sale to a foreign customer and the sales terms call for payment with a foreign currency, the company must translate the foreign currency into dollars to record the receivable. If the exchange rate changes before payment is received, foreign exchange gains or losses are recognized in the year in which they occur. The same treatment is used if a U.S. company makes a credit purchase from a foreign supplier and is required to make payment in a foreign currency. Also, if a U.S. company has a foreign subsidiary that maintains its accounts in a foreign currency, the account balances must be translated into dollars before they can be consolidated with the parent's accounts.

Learning Objective 5:

Explain the use of return on total assets in evaluating a company's efficiency in using its assets.

Summary

Return on total assets is used along with other ratios such as total asset turnover to evaluate the efficiency of a company in using its assets. Return on total assets is usually calculated as the annual net income divided by the average amount of total assets.

Learning Objective 6:

Define or explain the words and phrases listed in the chapter glossary.

Summary

See Problem III.

Topical Outline

I.   Natural resources—inventories of raw materials that will be converted into a product by cutting, mining, or pumping.

   A. Shown on the balance sheet at cost less accumulated depletion.

   B. Depletion is normally caluclated on a "units-of-production" basis.

II. Intangible assets—assets representing certain legal rights and economic relationships. They have no physical existence but are beneficial to the owner; patents, copyrights, leaseholds, leasehold improvements, trademarks, trade names, and goodwill.

   A. Recorded at cost and then amortized over its estimated useful life.

   B. Amortization period cannot exceed 40 years.

III. Investments in securities

   A. Short-term investments—investments that are expected to be converted into cash within one year or the current operating cycle of the business, whichever is longer; classified as current assets.

   B. Long-term investments—investments in stocks and bonds that are not marketable or, if marketable, are not intended to be a ready source of cash; classified as noncurrent assets. Investments are recorded at cost at the time of purchase.

      1. Debt securities held to maturity—owner must have the positive intent and ability to hold them until maturity. Investments are reported at original cost adjusted for amortization of any difference between cost and maturity value (cost method).

      2. Debt and equity securities available for sale. Regarding equity securities, the investor does not have significant influence (usually owns less than 20% of voting stock).

         a. Investments are reported at fair value (fair value method).

         b. Unrealized holding gains or losses are reported in the stockholders' equity section of the balance sheet.

      3. Equity securities which give the investor significant influence over the investee (owns more than 20%, but less than 50% of voting stock). Reported at cost plus share of undistributed earnings accumulated since purchase (equity method).

      4. Equity securities which give the investor control over the investee (owns more than 50% of voting stock).

         a. Parent company uses equity method in accounting records.

         b. Parent company reports to the public in consolidated financial statements.

IV. Accounting for international operations

   A. Multinational businesses are those having operations in several different countries.

   B. Foreign exchange rate—the price of one currency stated in terms of another currency.

   C. Sales or purchases denominated in a foreign currency.

      1. Companies making cash sales (or purchases) for which they receive (or pay) foreign currency must translate the transaction amounts into domestic currency.

      2. Receivables or payables stated in terms of foreign currencies result in exchange gains or losses as the foreign exchange rates fluctuate.

D. Consolidated statements with foreign subsidiaries—prepared using foreign exchange rates to translate the financial statements of the foreign subsidiaries into domestic currency.

V. Return on total assets

  A. A measure of a company's operating efficiency.

  B. Calculated as: $\dfrac{\text{Net income}}{\text{Average total assets}}$

Problem I

The following statements are either true or false. Place a (T) in the parentheses before each true statement and an (F) before each false statement.

1. ( ) Natural resources appear on the balance sheet at cost less accumulated depreciation.

2. ( ) The depletion cost of any mined but unsold natural resources which are held for sale is carried forward on the balance sheet as a current asset.

3. ( ) Trademarks and organization costs are intangible assets and must be amortized over the asset's useful life (not to exceed 40 years).

4. ( ) The amortization entry for the costs of leasehold improvements would debit Rent Expense and credit Leasehold Improvements.

5. ( ) Based on a given rate of return of 10%, the goodwill of a company that earns $25,000 annually, of which $5,000 is above-average earnings, should be estimated at $200,000.

6. ( ) The cost of all intangible assets must be amortized over 40 years.

7. ( ) An investor who owns 20% or more of a corporation's voting stock is presumed to have significant influence over the investee.

8. ( ) Unrealized holding gains and losses on investments in equity securities available for sale are reported in the stockholders' equity section of the balance sheet.

9. ( ) The equity method is used to account for investments in equity securities available for sale.

10. ( ) Under the cost method, when an investment in stock is sold and the proceeds net of any sales commission differ from cost, a gain or loss must be recorded.

11. ( ) At acquisition, the purchase of stock is recorded at cost regardless of which method is used to account for the investment.

12. ( ) The only difference between accounting for debt securities held to maturity and debt securities available for sale is that interest is not accrued on debt securities held to maturity.

13. ( ) Investments in equity securities available for sale are reported on the balance sheet at their fair values.

14. ( ) A credit sale by a U.S. company to a foreign customer required to make payment in U.S. dollars may result in an exchange gain or loss to the U.S. company.

Problem II

You are given several words, phrases, or numbers to choose from in completing each of the following statements or in answering the following questions. In each case select the one that best completes the statement or answers the question and place its letter in the answer space provided.

_____ 1. On January 1, 19X1, Allred Company purchased 12,000 shares of Moore Corporation's common stock at 60-1/4 plus a $6,000 commission. On July 1, 19X1, Moore Corporation declared and paid dividends of $0.85 per share, and on December 31, 19X1, it reported a net income of $156,000. Assuming Moore Corporation has 48,000 outstanding common shares and that the market value per share at December 31, 19X1, is $65, what is the carrying value of Allred's investment in Moore at December 31?

    a. $729,000.
    b. $757,800.
    c. $751,800.
    d. $723,000.
    e. $780,000.

_____ 2. On January 1, 19X1, Allred Company purchased 12,000 shares of Moore Corporation's common stock at 60-1/4 plus a $6,000 commission. On July 1, 19X1, Moore Corporation declared and paid dividends of $0.85 per share, and on December 31, 19X1, it reported a net income of $156,000. Assuming Moore Corporation has 96,000 outstanding common shares and that the market value per share at December 31, 19X1, is $65, what is the carrying value of Allred's investment in Moore at December 31?

    a. $723,000.
    b. $742,500.
    c. $738,300.
    d. $780,000.
    e. $729,000.

_____ 3. The process of allocating the cost of a patent to expense over time:

    a. Is called depletion.
    b. Is sometimes called depreciation.
    c. Is usually done by the declining-balance method over 50 years.
    d. Is seldom limited to less than 40 years.
    e. Should be accomplished in 17 years or less.

_____ 4. On December 1, Sprocket Company made a credit sale of 340,000 francs to Blanc Company of Paris, France, payment to be received in full on February 1. On December 1, the exchange rate for francs was $0.16420. On December 31, the exchange rate was $0.15930. Sprocket's December 31 adjusting entry to record the foreign exchange gain or loss would include a:

    a. $54,162 debit to Accounts Receivable.
    b. $1,666 credit to Foreign Exchange Gain or Loss.
    c. $1,666 debit to Accounts Receivable.
    d. $1,666 debit to Foreign Exchange Gain or Loss.
    e. No entry is made to record any foreign exchange gain or loss until actual payment is received on February 1.

_____ 5. Macon Company's total assets on December 31, 19X2 and 19X1, were $860,000 and $650,000, respectively. Net income for 19X2 was $77,400 and $42,250 for 19X1. Calculate Macon's return on total assets for 19X2.

    a. 9.0%.
    b. 10.3%.
    c. 7.0%.
    d. 7.9%.
    e. 6.5%.

Problem III

Many of the important ideas and concepts discussed in Chapter 11 are reflected in the following list of key terms. Test your understanding of these terms by matching the appropriate definitions with the terms. Record the number identifying the most appropriate definition in the blank space next to each term.

_____ Amortization	_____ Lessee
_____ Consolidated financial statements	_____ Lessor
_____ Copyright	_____ Long-term investments
_____ Depletion	_____ Multinational business
_____ Equity method	_____ Parent company
_____ Foreign exchange rate	_____ Patent
_____ Goodwill	_____ Reporting currency
_____ Intangible asset	_____ Return on total assets
_____ Lease	_____ Subsidiary
_____ Leasehold	_____ Trademark
_____ Leasehold improvements	_____ Trade name

1. The cost created by consuming the usefulness of natural resources.

2. The rights granted to a lessee by the lessor under the terms of a lease contract.

3. The process of systematically writing off the cost of an intangible asset to expense over its estimated useful life.

4. The price of one currency stated in terms of another currency.

5. Investments in stocks and bonds that are not marketable or, if marketable, are not intended to be a ready source of cash in case of need; also funds earmarked for a special purpose, such as bond sinking funds, and land or other assets not used in regular operations.

6. A company that operates in a large number of different countries.

7. An asset representing certain legal rights and economic relationships; it has no physical existence but is beneficial to the owner.

8. A measure of a company's operating efficiency, calculated by expressing net income as a percentage of average total assets.

9. A corporation that owns a controlling interest in another corporation (more than 50% of the voting stock is required).

10. Exclusive right granted by the federal government to manufacture and sell a patented machine or device, or to use a process, for 17 years.

11. An accounting method used when the investor has influence over the investee; the investment account is initially debited for cost and then is increased to reflect the investor's share of the investee's earnings and decreased to reflect the investor's receipt of dividends paid by the investee.

12. A corporation that is controlled by another corporation (the parent) because the parent owns more than 50% of the subsidiary's voting stock.

13. Improvements to leased property made and paid for by the lessee.

14. The currency in which a company presents its financial statements.

15. An exclusive right granted by the federal government or by international agreement to publish and sell a musical, literary, or artistic work for a period of years.

16. A unique name used by a company in marketing its products or services.

17. A unique symbol used by a company in marketing its products or services.

18. The individual or company that acquires the right to use property under the terms of a lease.

19. An intangible asset of a business that represents future earnings greater than the average in its industry; recognized in the financial statements only when a business is acquired at a price in excess of the fair market value of its net assets (excluding goodwill).

20. A contract under which the owner of property (the lessor) grants to a lessee the right to use the property.

21. The individual or company that owns property to be used by a lessee under the terms of a lease.

22. Financial statements that show the results of all operations under the parent's control, including those of any subsidiaries; assets and liabilities of all affiliated companies are combined on a single balance sheet, revenues and expenses are combined on a single income statement, and cash flows are combined on a single statement of cash flows as though the business were in fact a single company.

Problem IV

Complete the following by filling in the blanks.

1. If a corporation acquires _____ of another corporation's common stock, the investor is presumed to have a significant influence on the investee coporation's operations, and the investment should be accounted for according to the

   _____ .

2. Debt securities held to maturity should be accounted for according to the _____ ,

   _____ whereas debt securities available for sale should be accounted for according to the

   _____ .

3. Any entries to Foreign Exchange Gain or Loss on foreign currency transactions are closed to ___

   _____ and included on the _____ .

Problem V

On January 1, 19X1, Large Company paid $90,000 for 36,000 of Small Company's 90,000 outstanding common shares. Small Company paid a dividend of $20,000 on November 1, 19X1, and at the end of the year reported earnings of $40,000. The market value per share on December 31, 19X1, was $2.10. On January 3, 19X2, Large Company sold its interest in Small Company for $120,000.

1. What method should be used in Large Company's books to account for the investment in Small Company?

   _____

2. Complete general journal entries for Large Company to record the facts presented above. Do not give explanations and skip a line between entries.

DATE	ACCOUNT TITLES AND EXPLANATION	P.R.	DEBIT	CREDIT

Problem VI

On January 1, 19X1, Celestial Company paid $25,000 for 20,000 of Yardley Company's 120,000 outstanding common shares. Yardley Company paid a dividend of $.10 per share on June 1, 19X1, and at the end of the year reported earnings of $500,000. The market value per share on December 31, 19X1, was $1.90. Assume that Celestial did not own any investments prior to 19X1. On January 1, 19X2, Celestial Company sold its interest in Yardley Company for $37,900.

1. What method should be used by Celestial to account for its long-term investment in Yardley?

    _____

2. Complete general journal entries for Celestial Company to record the facts presented above. Also, prepare an entry dated January 1, 19X1, to remove any balances related to the fair value adjustment. Do not give explanations and skip a line between entries.

GENERAL JOURNAL
Page 1

DATE	ACCOUNT TITLES AND EXPLANATION	P.R.	DEBIT	CREDIT

Solutions for Chapter 11

Problem I

1.	F	8.	T
2.	T	9.	F
3.	T	10.	T
4.	T	11.	T
5.	F	12.	F
6.	F	13.	T
7.	T	14.	F

Problem II

1. B
2. D
3. E
4. D
5. B

Problem III

Problem IV

1. more than 20%, but less than 50%, equity method

2. cost method, fair value method

3. Income Summary, income statement

Problem V

1. The equity method

2. 19X1

Jan. 1	Investment in Small Company	90,000.00	
	Cash		90,000.00
Nov. 1	Cash	8,000.00	
	Investment in Small Company		8,000.00
Dec. 31	Investment in Small Company	16,000.00	
	Earnings from Investment in Small Company		16,000.00

19X2

Jan. 3	Cash	120,000.00	
	Investment in Small Company		98,000.00
	Gain on Sale of Investments		22,000.00

Problem VI

1. The fair value method

2.   19X1

Date		Account	Debit	Credit
Jan.	1	Investment in Yardley Company	25,000.00	
		Cash		25,000.00
June	1	Cash	2,000.00	
		Dividends Earned		2,000.00
Dec.	31	Long-Term Investments, Fair Value Adjustment	13,000.00	
		Unrealized Gain (Loss)		13,000.00

   19X2

Date		Account	Debit	Credit
Jan.	1	Cash	37,900.00	
		Investment in Yardley Company		25,000.00
		Gain on Sale of Investments		12,900.00
	1	Unrealized Gain (Loss)	13,000.00	
		Long-Term Investments, Fair Value Adjustment		13,000.00

12 Current and Long-Term Liabilities

Learning Objective 1:

Define liabilities, explain the difference between current and long-term liabilities, and describe the uncertainties related to some liabilities.

Summary

Liabilities are probable future payments of assets or services that an entity is presently obligated to make as a result of past events. Current liabilities are due within one year or one operating cycle, whichever is longer. All other liabilities are long-term liabilities. Potential uncertainties about a liability include the identity of the creditor, the due date, and the amount to be paid.

Learning Objective 2:

Describe how accountants record and report estimated liabilities such as warranties and income taxes, and how they report contingent liabilities.

Summary

If an uncertain future payment depends on a probable future event and the amount can be reasonably estimated, the payment should be reported as a liability. The future payment must be described as a contingent liability if *(a)* the future event is reasonably possible but not probable, or *(b)* the event is probable but the amount of the payment cannot be reasonably estimated.

Liabilities for warranties and income taxes are recorded with estimated amounts to be paid. This practice recognizes the expenses in the time period that they are incurred. Deferred income tax liabilities are recognized if temporary differences between GAAP and tax rules result in recording more income tax expense than the amount to be currently paid.

Learning Objective 3:

Describe payroll expenses and liabilities and prepare journal entries to account for them..

Summary

An employer's payroll expenses include gross earnings of the employees, additional employee benefits, and payroll taxes levied against the employer. Payroll liabilities include the net pay of employees, amounts withheld from the employees' wages, employee benefits, and the employer's payroll taxes. Payroll taxes are assessed for Social Security, Medicare, and unemployment programs.

Learning Objective 4:

Describe how accountants record and report short-term notes payable.

Summary

Short-term notes payable may be interest-bearing, in which case the face value of the note equals the amount borrowed and the note specifies a rate of interest to be paid until maturity. Noninterest-bearing notes include interest in their face value; thus, the face value equals the amount to be paid when the note matures.

Learning Objective 5:

Explain and calculate the present value of an amount to be paid at a future date and the present value of a series of equal amounts to be paid at future dates.

Summary

The primary present value concept is that today's value of an amount of cash to be paid or received in the future is less than today's value of the same amount of cash to be paid or received today. Another present value concept is that interest is compounded, which means that the interest is added to the balance and used to determine interest for succeeding periods. An annuity is a series of equal payments occurring at equal time intervals.

Learning Objective 6:

Describe how accountants use present value concepts in accounting for long-term notes, and how liabilities may result from leasing assets.

Summary

Accountants use present value concepts to determine the fair value of assets purchased in return for issuing debt. They also use present value concepts to allocate interest expense among the periods in a note's life by multiplying the note's beginning-of-period balance by the original interest rate. Noninterest-bearing notes are normally recorded with a discount account that is contra to the liability account. The balance of the discount account is amortized in the process of recognizing interest expense over the note's life.

Leases are an alternative to purchases as a means of gaining the use of assets. Capital leases give the lessee essentially the same risks and potential rewards as ownership. As a result, the leases and related leased obligations are recorded as assets and liabilities. Other leases, which are called operating leases, involve recording rent expense as the asset is used.

Learning Objective 7:

Calculate the number of times a company earns its fixed interest charges and describe what it reveals about a company's situation.

Summary

Times fixed interest charges earned is calculated by dividing a company's net income before interest by the amount of fixed interest charges incurred. This ratio describes the cushion that exists to protect the company's ability to pay interest and earn a profit for its owners against declines in its sales.

Learning Objective 8:

Define or explain the words and phrases listed in the chapter glossary.

Summary

See Problem III.

Topical Outline

  I. Definition and classification of liabilities

     A. Liabilities—present obligations that require the future payment of assets or performance of services because of a past event.

     B. Current liabilities—expected to be liquidated by using existing current assets or creating other current liabilities; due within one year of the balance sheet date or within the operating cycle of the business, whichever is longer.

     C. Long-term liabilities—do not require the use of existing current assets because they do not mature within one year or the current operating cycle, whichever is longer.

     D. Liabilities and uncertainty—liabilities may be uncertain with respect to:

        1. Identity of the creditor.

        2. Due date.

        3. Amount (in which case the liability is called an estimated liability).

     E. Estimated liabilities—obligations that exist but have an uncertain amount that can be estimated. Examples are:

        1. Warranty liabilities.

        2. Income tax liabilities on interim statements.

        3. Deferred income tax liabilities.

     F. Contingent liabilities—possible obligations reported in footnotes because of uncertainty about their existence, amount, or both. Examples are:

        1. Potential legal claims.

        2. Debt guarantees.

  II. Payroll liabilities

     A. Federal Insurance Contribution Act (FICA) taxes—also known as Social Security and Medicare taxes, are levied on the employer and the employee in equal amounts.

     B. Federal income taxes levied on employees must be withheld by employers.

     C. Other deductions from wages—charitable contributions, health insurance premiums, union dues.

     D. State and federal unemployment taxes are levied on employers.

     E. Employee benefit costs are expenses that must be accrued along with other payroll costs.

     F. Expenses related to vacation pay should be estimated and recorded by the employer during the weeks the employees are working and earning the vacation time.

 III. Short-term notes payable

     A. Examples

        1. Note given to secure a time extension on an account.

        2. Note given to secure a loan from a bank.

           a. Discount on note payable—the difference between the amount borrowed and the face value of the note.

           b. Noninterest-bearing note—a note that does not have a stated rate of interest.

B. End-of-period adjustments

    1. Accrued interest expense on outstanding notes payable should be recorded at the end of the accounting period.

    2. Interest on a discounted note must be allocated to the periods benefited.

IV. Present value

    A. The concept: a dollar to be received or paid in the future has less value than a dollar received or paid today.

    B. Present value tables—used instead of formulas to solve present value problems.
        1. "Present value of $1" table used for problem based on single payments.

        2. "Present value of an annuity of $1" table used for problem based on a number of equal payments.

        3. Interest rates are normally expressed in annual amounts.

        4. Discount periods can be any length of time; if less than a year, annual interest rate must be adjusted for the discount period.

V. Issuing a note to buy a plant asset

    A. Asset should be recorded at its fair value or at the present value of the note, whichever is more clearly determinable.

    B. A discount on a note payable is created if the note does not have a stated interest rate or if the interest rate is unreasonably low. The discount is amortized over the life of the note.

VI. Liabilities from leasing

    A. Capital lease—gives a lessee the risks and benefits normally associated with ownership. The lessee reports both a leased asset and a lease liability.

    B. Operating lease—a lease that is not a capital lease. The lessee reports rent expense.

VII. Times fixed interest charges earned

    A. Used to describe the risk created by variable amounts of income.

    B. Calculated as: $\dfrac{\text{Income before interest}}{\text{Interest expense}}$

Problem I

The following statements are either true or false. Place a (T) in the parentheses before each true statement and an (F) before each false statement.

1. ( ) An example of an estimated liability is a warranty.

2. ( ) Contingent liabilities are generally not recognized on the balance sheet.

3. ( ) When a borrower records the cash proceeds from a noninterest-bearing note payable, Discount on Notes Payable may be debited for the amount of interest included in the face amount of the note by the lender.

4. ( ) The borrower is required to pay the lender the face amount of the note when a noninterest-bearing note matures.

5. ( ) The concept of present value is based on the idea that the right to receive $1 a year from now is worth more than $1 today.

6. ( ) Receiving $500 on June 30 and $500 on December 31 has the same present value as receiving $1,000 on December 31.

7. ( ) If a note requires quarterly payments and the borrower could obtain a 12% annual rate of interest in borrowing money, a 3% quarterly interest rate should be used to determine the present value of the note.

8. ( ) A discount on a note payable is a contra liability.

9. ( ) The carrying amount of a payable decreases each year by the amount of discount amortized that year.

10. ( ) The process of allocating the interest on a noninterest-bearing note payable is called amortizing the discount.

11. ( ) Depending on the terms of a lease obligation, the lease may or may not be recorded as a liability.

12. ( ) Depreciation is recorded on a machine obtained under a capital lease.

13. ( ) A corporation would report a deferred income tax liability when reported income tax expense for the year is greater than the amount of tax actually paid.

14. ( ) Federal unemployment taxes are withheld from employees' wages at the rate of 1.45% on the first $61,200 earned.

15. ( ) Social Security taxes are levied equally on the employee and the employer.

16. ( ) Employee benefit costs represent expenses to the employer in addition to the direct costs of salaries and wages.

17. ( ) Each time a payroll is recorded, a separate journal entry usually is made to record the employer's FICA and state and federal unemployment taxes.

18. ( ) Since federal income taxes withheld from an employee's wages are expenses of the employee, not the employer, they should not be treated as liabilities of the employer.

19. ( ) Since Jon Company has very little employee turnover, the company has received a very favorable merit rating. As a result, Jon Company should expect to pay substantially smaller amounts of FICA taxes than normal.

20. ( ) Select Company's income before interest is $292,400 and interest expense is $86,000. Select's times fixed interest charges earned is 3.4 times.

Problem II

You are given several words, phrases, or numbers to choose from in completing each of the following statements or in answering the following questions. In each case select the one that best completes the statement or answers the question and place its letter in the answer space provided.

_____ 1. On November 1, 19X1, Profitable Company borrowed $50,000 by giving a 90-day, 12% note payable. The company has an annual, calendar-year accounting period and does not make reversing entries. What amount should be debited to Interest Expense on January 30, 19X2?

     a. $6,000.
     b. $1,500.
     c. $1,000.
     d. $ 500.
     e. $ 0.

_____ 2. Indigo, Inc., is offered a contract whereby it will be paid $15,000 every six months for the next five years. The first payment will be received six months from today. What will the company be willing to pay for this contract if it expects a 16% annual return on the investment? [Use the appropriate present value table in the chapter in the text.]

     a. $ 10,209.00
     b. $ 6,948.00
     c. $100,651.50
     d. $ 59,890.50
     e. Cannot be determined from information provided.

Use the following information as to earnings and deductions for the pay period ended November 15 taken from a company's payroll records for the next two questions:

Employee's Name	Earnings to End of Previous Week	Gross Pay This Week	Federal Income Taxes	Medical Insurance Deducted
Rita Hawn	$25,700	$ 800	$155.00	$ 35.50
Dolores Hopkins	930	800	134.00	35.50
Robert Allen	65,900	1,000	193.00	42.00
Calvin Ingram	18,400	740	128.00	42.00
		$3,340	$610.00	$155.00

_____ 3. Employees' FICA taxes are withheld at an assumed rate of 6.2% on the first $66,000 earned for Social Security and 1.45% of all wages earned for Medicare. The journal entry to accrue the payroll should include a:

     a. Debit to Accrued Payroll Payable for $3,340.
     b. Debit to FICA Taxes Payable for $255.51.
     c. Debit to Payroll Taxes Expense for $765.
     d. Credit to FICA Taxes Payable for $199.71.
     e. Credit to Accrued Payroll Payable for $2,575.

_____ 4. Assume a state unemployment tax rate of 2% on the first $7,000 paid each employee and a federal unemployment tax rate of 0.8% on the first $7,000 paid each employee. The journal entry to record the employer's payroll taxes resulting from the payroll should include a debit to Payroll Taxes Expense for:

     a. $222.11
     b. $277.91
     c. $293.23
     d. $349.03
     e. The entry does not include a debit to Payroll Taxes Expense.

Problem III

Many of the important ideas and concepts that are discussed in Chapter 12 are reflected in the following list of key terms. Test your understanding of these terms by matching the appropriate definitions with the terms. Record the number identifying the most appropriate definition in the blank space next to each term.

_____ Annuity

_____ Capital lease

_____ Deferred income tax liability

_____ Discount on note payable

_____ Employee benefits

_____ Estimated liability

_____ FICA taxes

_____ Merit rating

_____ Noninterest-bearing note

_____ Operating lease

_____ Present value

_____ Present value table

_____ Times fixed interest charges earned

_____ Warranty

1. Payments of income taxes that are deferred until future years because of temporary differences between GAAP and tax rules.

2. An obligation that is reported as a liability even though the amount to be paid is uncertain.

3. A series of equal payments occurring at equal time intervals.

4. A note that does not have a stated rate of interest; the interest is included in the face value of the note.

5. The difference between the face value of a noninterest-bearing note payable and the amount borrowed; represents interest that will be paid on the note over its life.

6. The amount that can be invested (borrowed) at a given interest rate to generate a total future investment (debt) that will equal the amount of a specified future receipt (payment).

7. A table that shows the present values of an amount to be received when discounted at various interest rates for various periods of time, or the present values of a series of equal payments to be received for a varying number of periods when discounted at various interest rates.

8. A lease that gives the lessee the risks and benefits normally associated with ownership.

9. Taxes assessed on both employers and employees under the Federal Insurance Contributions Act; these taxes fund Social Security and Medicare programs.

10. The ratio of a company's income before interest divided by the amount of interest charges; used to evaluate the risk of being committed to make interest payments when income varies.

11. An agreement that obligates the seller or manufacturer to repair or replace a product within a specified period.

12. A lease that is not a capital lease.

13. A rating assigned to an employer by a state according to the employer's past record for creating or not creating unemployment; a higher rating produces a lower unemployment tax rate.

14. Additional compensation paid to or on behalf of employees, such as premiums for medical, dental, life, and disability insurance, contributions to pension plans, and vacations.

Problem IV

Complete the following by filling in the blanks.

1. Use the present value tables in the text to calculate the following present values:

   a. $1 to be received 9 years hence, at 10%. $_____

   b. $2,000 to be received 6 years hence, at 8%. $_____

   c. $1 to be received at the end of each year for 10 years, at 4%.

      $_____

   d. $1,000 to be received at the end of each year for 7 years, at 6%.

      $_____

2. A debt guarantee is an example of a _____ liability.

3. When the rate of interest on an investment is 8% compounded annually, the present value of $1,000 to be received three years hence is the amount of money that must be invested today that together with

   the 8% compound interest earned on the investment will equal $_____

   at the end of three years. The amount is $1,000 x $_____ = $_____.

4. When the account Discount on Notes Payable is shown on the balance sheet, does it increase or decrease the carrying amount of Notes Payable?

   _____

5. Certain leases require the lessee to report a leased asset and a lease liability. These leases are known

   as _____.

6. If the interest rate is changed from 5% to 8%, will the present value of $1 to be received in one year be increased or decreased?

   _____

7. Good employer merit ratings give employers a reduction in their state unemployment tax rates as a reward for

   _____.

8. The two components of FICA taxes are _____ and
   _____.

9. Employers pay FICA taxes _____ to those withheld from employees.

Problem V

Glitz Company estimates that future costs to satisfy its product warranty obligation amount to 3% of sales. In January, the company sold merchandise for $50,000 cash and paid $1,200 to repair products returned for warranty work. Present the journal entries related to the product warranty.

DATE	ACCOUNT TITLES AND EXPLANATION	P.R.	DEBIT	CREDIT

Problem VI

A company whose accounting periods end each December 31 borrowed $10,000 at 12% for 60 days by signing a note on December 16, 19X1. The face value of the note includes both the principal and interest. Complete the following entries involving this note.

DATE	ACCOUNT TITLES AND EXPLANATION	P.R.	DEBIT	CREDIT
19X1				
Dec. 16				
	Borrowed cash with a 60 day, 12% note.			
31				
	To record interest on note payable.			
19X2				
Feb. 14				
	To pay note with interest.			

Problem VII

Assume that on January 2, 19X1, a day on which the prevailing interest rate was 8%, a company exchanged a $15,000, five-year, noninterest-bearing note payable for a machine, the cash price of which was not readily determinable.

1. The present value of the note on the day of exchange and the amount at which the machine should be recorded is calculated:

   $15,000 x $ _____ = $ _____.

2. The entry to record the exchange is:

DATE	ACCOUNT TITLES AND EXPLANATION	P.R.	DEBIT	CREDIT

3. The amount of discount to be amortized at the end of the first year in the five-year life of the note is calculated:

   $ _____ x 8% = $ _____.

4. The discount amortization entry at the end of the first year is:

DATE	ACCOUNT TITLES AND EXPLANATION	P.R.	DEBIT	CREDIT

5. The note should appear on the company's balance sheet at the end of its first year as follows:

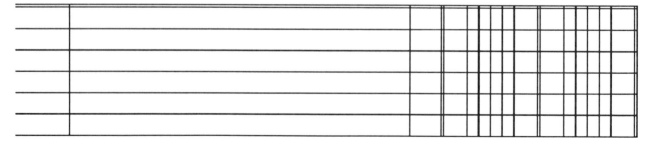

Problem VIII

The following information as to earnings and deductions for the pay period ended November 15 was taken from a company's payroll records:

Employee's Name	Earnings to End of Previous Week	Gross Pay This Week	Federal Income Taxes	Hospital Insurance Deducted
Rita Hawn	$25,700	$ 800	$155.00	$ 35.50
Dolores Hopkins	930	800	134.00	35.50
Robert Allen	65,900	1,000	193.00	42.00
Calvin Ingram	18,400	740	128.00	42.00
		$3,340	$610.00	$155.00

Required:

1. Calculate the employees' FICA taxes withheld assuming a rate of 6.2% on the first $66,000 earned for Social Security and 1.45% of all wages earned for Medicare, and prepare a journal entry to accrue the payroll under the assumption that all of the employees work in the office.

2. Prepare a journal entry to record the employer's payroll taxes resulting from the payroll. Assume a state unemployment tax rate of 2% on the first $7,000 paid each employee and a federal unemployment tax rate of 0.8% on the first $7,000 paid each employee.

DATE	ACCOUNT TITLES AND EXPLANATION	P.R.	DEBIT	CREDIT

Solutions for Chapter 12

Problem I

1. T	11. T
2. T	12. T
3. T	13. T
4. T	14. F
5. F	15. T
6. F	16. T
7. T	17. T
8. T	18. F
9. F	19. F
10. T	20. T

Problem II

1. D
2. C
3. D
4. A

Problem III

Annuity	3	Merit rating	13
Capital lease	8	Noninterest-bearing note	4
Deferred income tax liability	1	Operating lease	12
Discount on note payable	5	Present value	6
Employee benefits	14	Present value table	7
Estimated liability	2	Times fixed interest charges earned	10
FICA taxes	9	Warranty	11

Problem IV

1. a. $0.4241
    b. $2,000 x 0.6302 = $1,260.40
    c. $8.1109
    d. $1,000 x $5.5824 = $5,582.40

2. contingent

3. $1,000, $1,000 x $0.7938 = $793.80

4. decrease

5. capital leases

6. decreased

7. providing stable employment for employees

8. Social Security taxes, Medicare taxes

9. equal

Problem V

Jan. —	Warranty Expense ($50,000 x 0.03)	1,500.00	
	Estimated Warranty Liability		1,500.00
—	Estimated Warranty Liability	1,200.00	
	Cash		1,200.00

Problem VI

19X1

Dec. 16	Cash	10,000.00	
	Discount on Notes Payable	200.00	
	Notes Payable		10,200.00
31	Interest Expense	50.00	
	Discount on Notes Payable		50.00

19X2

Feb. 14	Interest Expense	150.00	
	Notes Payable	10,200.00	
	Discount on Notes Payable		150.00
	Cash		10,200.00

Problem VII

1. $15,000 x $0.6806 = $10,209

2.

Jan. 2	Machinery	10,209.00	
	Discount on Notes Payable	4,791.00	
	Long-Term Notes Payable		15,000.00

3. $10,209 x 8% = $816.72

4.

Dec. 31	Interest Expense	816.72	
	Discount on Notes Payable		816.72

5. Long-term liabilities:

Long-term note payable	$15,000.00
Less discount	3,974.28*
Net liability	$11,025.72

*$4,791.00 - $816.72 = $3,974.28

Problem VIII

Nov. 15	Office Salaries Expense	3,340.00	
	FICA Taxes Payable		199.71
	Employees' Federal Income Taxes Payable		610.00
	Employees' Hospital Insurance Payable		155.00
	Accrued Payroll Payable		2,375.29

($800 + $800 + $100 + $740) x .062 = $151.28
$3,340 x .0145 = $48.43
$151.28 + $48.43 = $199.71

15	Payroll Taxes Expense	222.11	
	FICA Taxes Payable		199.71
	State Unemployment Taxes Payable		16.00
	Federal Unemployment Taxes Payable		6.40

$800 x 0.02 = $16
$800 x 0.008 = $6.40

C   Payroll Reports, Records, and Procedures

Learning Objective 1:

Describe an employer's payroll reports and records, and the procedures used to calculate tax withholdings and issue checks to employees.

Summary

Employers report FICA taxes and federal income tax withholdings quarterly on Form 941. FUTA taxes are reported annually on Form 940. Annual earnings and deduction information are reported to each employee and to the federal government on Form W-2. An employer's payroll records include a Payroll Register for each pay period and an Employee's Individual Earnings Record for each employee.

Federal income tax withholdings depend on the employee's earnings and the number of withholding allowances claimed by the employee. Various wage bracket withholding tables are available for pay periods of different lengths and for several classes of employees such as single or married.

Employers with a large number of employees often use a separate payroll bank account. When this is done, the payment of employees is recorded with a single credit to Cash. This entry records the transfer of cash from the regular checking account to the payroll checking account.

Learning Objective 2:

Define or explain the words and phrases listed in the appendix glossary.

Summary

See Problem II.

Topical Outline

I. Reports to be completed and filed by the employer include:

    A. Employer's Quarterly Federal Tax Return (Form 941).

    B. Wage and Tax Statement (Form W-2).

II. Maintaining payroll records

    A. Payroll Register—a record for a pay period that shows the pay period dates and the hours worked, gross pay, deductions, and net pay of each employee; contains all the data needed to record payroll (for each pay period) in the General Journal.

    B. Employee's Individual Earnings Record—a record of an employee's hours worked, gross pay, deductions, net pay, and certain personal information about the employee; contains the data the employer needs to prepare a Form W-2.

    C. Federal income tax withholdings

        1. Withholding allowances—a number that is used to reduce the amount of federal income tax withheld from an employee's pay, and which corresponds to the personal exemptions the employee is allowed to subtract from annual earnings in calculating taxable income; indicated by each employee on withholding allowance certificate (Form W-4).

        2. Wage bracket withholding table—a table that shows the amounts of income tax to be withheld from the employees' wages at various levels of earnings.

    D. Payments to employees are made:

        1. From a regular bank account in a company with few employees.

        2. Through a separate payroll bank account in a company with many employees.

Problem I

The following statements are either true or false. Place a (T) in the parentheses before each true statement and an (F) before each false statement.

1. ( ) An employer's FICA taxes are reported annually on a Form 940.

2. ( ) If an employer's total FUTA taxes for the year are $100 or less, the amount due may be remitted annually rather than quarterly.

3. ( ) As the number of withholding allowances claimed increases, the amount of income tax to be withheld increases.

4. ( ) A special payroll bank account is used to replenish the regular bank account after all the employees are paid.

Problem II

Many of the important ideas and concepts that are discussed in Appendix C are reflected in the following list of key terms. Test your understanding of these terms by matching the appropriate definitions with the terms. Record the number identifying the most appropriate definition in the blank space next to each term.

_____ Employee's Individual Earnings Record   _____ Payroll Register

_____ Federal depository bank   _____ Wage bracket withholding table

_____ Payroll bank account   _____ Withholding allowance

1. A record of an employee's hours worked, gross pay, deductions, net pay, and certain personal information about the employee.

2. A special bank account a company uses solely for the purpose of paying employees, by depositing in the account each pay period an amount equal to the total employees' net pay and drawing the employees' payroll checks on that account.

3. A number that is used to reduce the amount of federal income tax withheld from an employee's pay.

4. A record for a pay period that shows the pay period dates and the hours worked, gross pay, deductions, and net pay of each employee.

5. A bank authorized to accept deposits of amounts payable to the federal government.

6. A table that shows the amounts of income tax to be withheld from employees' wages at various levels of earnings.

Problem III

Complete the following by filling in the blanks.

1. According to law, a _____
   showing wages earned and taxes withheld must be given by the employer to each employee within one
   month after the year-end.

2. The amount to be withheld from an employee's wages for federal income taxes is determined by

   (a) _____

   and (b) _____ .

3. According to the wage bracket withholding table of Illustration C-5 in your text, $_____ should
   be withheld from the wages of an employee for federal income taxes if the employee has two exemptions
   and earned $860 in a week.

4. According to the Federal Insurance Contributions Act, an employer must file an Employer's Quarterly

   Federal Tax Return (Form _____) within one month after the end of each _____

   _____ .

5. The _____ contains all the data needed to prepare
   the general journal entry to record payroll.

6. An employee's working time, gross earnings, deductions, and net pay for a full year are summarized in an

   _____ .

Problem IV

The Payroll Register of Whiteman Sales for the first week of the year follows. The deductions and net pay of the first three employees have been calculated and entered.

1. Use an assumed 8% FICA tax rate (Medicare and Social Security have been combined for this problem) and complete the payroll information opposite the name of the last employee, Fred Clarke. In addition to FICA taxes, Mr. Clarke should have $111 of federal income taxes, $20 of medical insurance, and no union dues withheld from his wages, which are chargeable to office salaries. The overtime premium rate is 50%.

PAYROLL REGISTER

EMPLOYEE'S NAME	CLOCK CARD NUMBER	DAILY TIME M	T	W	T	F	S	S	TOTAL HOURS	O.T. HOURS	REG. PAY RATE		REGULAR PAY		O.T. PREMIUM PAY		GROSS PAY		
Delbert Landau	12	8	8	8	7	4	0	0	35		11	00	385	00			385	00	1
Maria Garza	9	8	8	8	5	4	0	0	33		12	00	396	00			396	00	2
Ralph Webster	15	8	8	7	8	4	0	0	35		13	00	455	00			455	00	3
Fred Clarke	4	8	8	8	8	8	4	0	44	4	14	00	616	00	28	00	644	00	4
																			5

Week ending January 8, 19—

	FICA TAXES		FEDERAL INCOME TAXES		HOSPITAL INSUR-ANCE		UNION DUES		TOTAL DEDUC-TIONS		NET PAY		CHECK NUMBER	SALES SALARIES		OFFICE SALARIES		DELIVERY WAGES	
1	30	80	65	00	20	00	10	00	125	80	259	20						385	00
2	31	68	63	00	20	00	10	00	124	68	271	32		396	00				
3	36	40	68	00	20	00	10	00	134	40	320	60		455	00				
4	51	52	111	00	20	00			182	52	461	48				644	00		
5																			

2. Complete the Payroll Register by totaling its columns, and give the general journal entry to record its information.

DATE	ACCOUNT TITLES AND EXPLANATION	P.R.	DEBIT	CREDIT

Whiteman Sales uses a special payroll bank account in paying its employees. Each payday, after the general journal entry recording the information of its Payroll Register is posted, a single check for the total of the employees' net pay is drawn and deposited in the payroll bank account. This transfers funds equal to the payroll total from the regular bank account to the payroll bank account. Then special payroll checks are written on the payroll bank account and given to the employees. For the January 8 payroll, four payroll checks beginning with payroll Check No. 102 were drawn and delivered to the employees. Record this information in the Payroll Register.

3. Make the entry to record the transfer of cash to the payroll bank account for the January 8 payroll.

DATE	ACCOUNT TITLES AND EXPLANATION	P.R.	DEBIT	CREDIT

4. Make the general journal entry to record the payroll taxes levied on Whiteman Sales as a result of the payroll entered in its January 8 Payroll Register. The company has a merit rating that reduces its state employment tax rate to 1% of the first $7,000 paid each employee. (The federal unemployment tax rate is 0.8%.)

DATE	ACCOUNT TITLES AND EXPLANATION	P.R.	DEBIT	CREDIT

5. The individual earnings record of Fred Clarke follows. Transfer from the Payroll Register to Mr. Clarke's earnings record the payroll data for the first pay period of the year.

EMPLOYEE'S INDIVIDUAL EARNINGS RECORD

EMPLOYEE'S NAME _____ Fred Clarke _____   S.S. NO. _____ 119-05-1879 _____   EMPLOYEE NO. _____ 4 _____

HOME ADDRESS _____ 2590 Columbia Street _____

NOTIFY IN CASE OF EMERGENCY _____ Mary Clarke _____   REASON _____

PHONE NUMBER _____ 965-5698 _____

EMPLOYED _____ 9/1/80 _____

DATE OF TERMINATION _____

DATE OF BIRTH _____ May 20, 1943 _____   DATE BECOMES 65 _____ May 20, 2008 _____

MALE (x) MARRIED (x)
FEMALE ( ) SINGLE ( )

NUMBER OF EXEMPTIONS _____ 4 _____

PAY RATE _____ $14.00 _____

OCCUPATION _____ Manager _____   PLACE _____ Store and office _____

DATE		TIME LOST		TIME WK.		REG. PAY	O.T. PREM. PAY	GROSS PAY	F.I.C.A. TAXES	FED. INC. TAXES	HOSPI-TAL INSUR-ANCE	UNION DUES	TOTAL DEDUC-TIONS	NET PAY	CHECK NUMBER	CUMU-LATIVE PAY
PER. ENDS	PAID	HRS.	REASON	TOTAL	O.T. HOURS										

Solutions for Appendix C

Problem I

1. F
2. T
3. F
4. F

Problem II

Problem III

1. Form W-2 (Wage and Tax Statement)
2. (a) the amount of his or her wages,
   (b) the number of his or her withholding allowances
3. $146
4. 941, calendar quarter
5. Payroll Register
6. Employee's Individual Earnings Record

Problem IV

1. and 2.

EMPLOYEE'S NAME	CLOCK CARD NUMBER	DAILY TIME							TOTAL HOURS	O.T. HOURS	REG. PAY RATE		EARNINGS						
		M	T	W	T	F	S	S					REGULAR PAY		O.T. PREMIUM PAY		GROSS PAY		
Delbert Landau	12	8	8	8	7	4	0	0	35		11	00	385	00			385	00	1
Maria Garza	9	8	8	8	5	4	0	0	33		12	00	396	00			396	00	2
Ralph Webster	15	8	8	7	8	4	0	0	35		13	00	455	00			455	00	3
Fred Clarke	4	8	8	8	8	8	4	0	44	4	14	00	616	00	28	00	644	00	4
													1,852	00	28	00	1,880	00	5

Week ending January 8, 19—

	DEDUCTIONS									PAYMENT			DISTRIBUTION					
	FICA TAXES		FEDERAL INCOME TAXES		HOSPITAL INSUR-ANCE		UNION DUES		TOTAL DEDUC-TIONS	NET PAY		CHECK NUMBER	SALES SALARIES		OFFICE SALARIES		DELIVERY WAGES	
1	30	80	65	00	20	00	10	00	125 80	259	20	102					385	00
2	31	68	63	00	20	00	10	00	124 68	271	32	103	396	00				
3	36	40	68	00	20	00	10	00	134 40	320	60	104	455	00				
4	51	52	111	00	20	00			182 52	461	48	105			644	00		
5	150	40	307	00	80	00	30	00	567 40	1,312	60		851	00	644	00	385	00

Jan. 8	Sales Salaries Expense	851.00	
	Office Salaries Expense	644.00	
	Delivery Wages Expense	385.00	
	FICA Taxes Payable		150.40
	Employees' Federal Income Taxes Payable		307.00
	Employees' Medical Insurance Payable		80.00
	Employees' Union Dues Payable		30.00
	Accrued Payroll Payable		1,312.60
3. Jan. 8	Accrued Payroll Payable	1,312.60	
	Cash		1,312.60
4. Jan. 8	Payroll Taxes Expense	184.24	
	FICA Taxes Payable		150.40
	State Unemployment Taxes Payable		18.80
	Federal Unemployment Taxes Payable		15.04

5.

EMPLOYEE'S INDIVIDUAL EARNINGS RECORD

EMPLOYEE'S NAME __Fred Clarke__   S.S. NO. __119-05-1879__   EMPLOYEE NO. __4__

HOME ADDRESS __2590 Columbia Street__

NOTIFY IN CASE OF EMERGENCY __Mary Clarke__   PHONE NUMBER __965-5698__

EMPLOYED __9/1/80__   DATE OF TERMINATION _____   REASON _____

DATE OF BIRTH __May 20, 1943__   DATE BECOMES 65 __May 20, 2008__

MALE ( ) MARRIED (x)   FEMALE (x) SINGLE ( )   NUMBER OF EXEMPTIONS __4__   PAY RATE __$14.00__

OCCUPATION __Manager__   PLACE __Store and office__

DATE		TIME LOST		TIME WK.		REG. PAY	O.T. PREM. PAY	GROSS PAY	F.I.C.A. TAXES	FED. INC. TAXES	HOSPI-TAL INSUR-ANCE	UNION DUES	TOTAL DEDUC-TIONS	NET PAY	CHECK NUMBER	CUMU-LATIVE PAY
PER. ENDS	PAID	HRS.	REASON	TOTAL	O.T. HOURS											
1/8	1/8			44	4	616 00	28 00	644 00	51 54	111 00	20 00		182 52	461 48	105	644 00

D Accounting Principles, the FASB's Conceptual Framework, and Alternative Valuation Methods

Learning Objective 1:

Explain the difference between descriptive concepts and prescriptive concepts, and the difference between bottom-up and top-down approaches to the development of accounting concepts.

Summary

Some accounting concepts provide general descriptions of current accounting practices and are most useful in learning about accounting. Other accounting concepts prescribe the practices accountants should follow. These prescriptive concepts are most useful in developing accounting procedures for new types of transactions and making improvements in accounting practice. A bottom-up approach to developing concepts begins by examining the practices currently in use. Then, concepts are developed that provide general descriptions of those practices. In contrast, a top-down approach begins by stating the objectives of accounting. From these objectives, concepts are developed that prescribe the types of accounting practices accountants should follow.

Learning Objective 2:

Describe the major components in the FASB's conceptual framework.

Summary

The FASB's conceptual framework begins with *SFAC 1* by stating the broad objectives of financial reporting. Next, *SFAC 2* identifies the qualitative characteristics accounting information should possess. The elements contained in financial reports are defined in *SFAC 6* and the recognition and measurement criteria to be used are identified in *SFAC 5*.

Learning Objective 3:

Explain why conventional financial statements fail to adequately account for price changes.

Summary

Conventional financial statements report transactions in terms of the historical number of dollars received or paid. Therefore, the statements are not adjusted to reflect general price level changes or changes in the specific prices of the items reported.

Learning Objective 4:

Use a price index to restate historical cost/nominal dollar costs into constant purchasing power amounts and to calculate purchasing power gains and losses.

Summary

To restate a historical cost/nominal dollar cost in constant purchasing power terms, multiply the nominal dollar cost by a factor that represents the change in the general price level since the cost was incurred. On the balance sheet, monetary assets and liabilities should not be adjusted for changes in prices. However, purchasing power gains or losses result from holding monetary assets and owing monetary liabilities during a period of general price changes.

Learning Objective 5:

Explain the current cost approach to valuation, including its effects on the income statement and balance sheet.

Summary

Current costs on the balance sheet are the dollar amounts that would be spent to purchase the assets at the balance sheet date. On the income statement, current costs are the dollar amounts that would be necessary to acquire the consumed assets on the date they were consumed.

Learning Objective 6:

Explain the current selling price approach to valuation.

Summary

Reporting current selling prices of assets and liabilities is supported by those who believe the balance sheet should show the net cost of not selling the assets and settling the liabilities. Some argue for applying selling price valuations to all assets and liabilities, or to marketable investments and marketable liabilities only, or to assets only. The related gains and losses may be reported on the income statement, but some would show them as unrealized stockholders' equity items on the balance sheet. The FASB's newly issued *SFAS 114* requires companies to use the selling price approach in reporting certain securities investments.

Learning Objective 7:

Define or explain the words and phrases listed in the appendix glossary.

Summary

See Problem III.

Topical Outline

I. Descriptive accounting concepts:

    A. Provide general descriptions of existing accounting practices.

    B. Serve as guidelines that help you learn about accounting.

    C. Generally accepted principles established prior to the FASB's conceptual framework are generally descriptive.

    D. Descriptive accounting principles established prior to the FASB's conceptual framework include:

        1. Business entity principle.

        2. Conservatism principle.

        3. Consistency principle.

        4. Cost principle.

        5. Full-disclosure principle.

        6. Going concern principle.

        7. Matching principle.

        8. Materiality principle.

        9. Objectivity principle.

        10. Revenue recognition principle.

        11. Time-period principle.

II. Prescriptive accounting concepts:

    A. Describe what should be done in practice, not necessarily what is done in practice.

    B. Help accountants analyze unfamiliar situations and develop procedures to account for those situations.

III. "Bottom-up" versus "top-down" approaches to establishing accounting concepts

    A. "Bottom-up" approach starts by observing existing accounting practices and then develops general concepts that describe those practices.

    B. "Top-down" approach starts with statement of objectives about what accounting should accomplish, then deduces general concepts of accounting that are consistent with the objectives, then identifies specific practices that are consistent with the general concepts.

IV. The FASB's conceptual framework project—intended to provide prescriptive concepts for financial reporting

    A. Contained in a series of FASB pronouncements called *Statements of Financial Accounting Concepts.*

    B. Stated objectives of financial reporting

        1. Financial reporting should provide information that is useful in making investment, credit, and similar decisions.

        2. Financial reporting should help users predict future cash flows.

        3. Information about a company's resources and obligations is useful.

C. Identified qualities of useful information

 1. Relevant.

 2. Reliable.

 3. Comparable.

D. Defined elements of financial statements—including categories such as assets, liabilities, equity, revenues, expenses, gains, and losses.

E. Specified criteria for recognition and measurement

 1. Items should be recognized in financial statements if they meet the following:

  a. Must meet definition of an element.

  b. Must have relevant attribute that is measurable with sufficient reliability.

  c. Information about item must be relevant or capable of making a difference in a user decision.

  d. Information must be reliable, or representationally faithful, verifiable, and neutral.

 2. A full set of financial statements should show:

  a. Financial position at the end of the period.

  b. Earnings for the period.

  c. Comprehensive income for the period.

  d. Cash flows during the period.

  e. Investments by and distributions to owners during the period.

V. Conventional financial statements and price changes

A. Balance sheet amounts are stated in nominal dollars and usually do not show the effects of price changes.

B. Expenses that are allocations of costs recorded in earlier periods are not stated in terms of current dollars.

VI. Historical costs adjusted for general price level changes

A. A general price index is used to restate historical cost/nominal dollar amounts so that they represent current general purchasing power.

B. Procedures involve:

 1. Calculating general purchasing power gains or losses from owning monetary assets or owing monetary liabilities.

 2. Adjusting nonmonetary items for price changes since the items were first purchased.

VII. Current replacement cost valuations

A. On the income statement, the current cost of an expense is the number of dollars needed to acquire the consumed resource at the time the expense was incurred.

B. Specific price indexes and other estimates are used to report current costs of nonmonetary balance sheet items at each balance sheet date.

VIII. Current selling price valuations

A. Assets and liabilities may be reported at their current selling prices, and stockholders' equity would represent the net cash that would be realized by liquidating the business.

B. Related gains and losses may be reported either on the income statement (which could cause large fluctuations in net income) or on the balance sheet as "unrealized" gains and losses.

Problem I

The following statements are either true or false. Place a (T) in the parentheses before each true statement and an (F) before each false statement.

1. ( ) Prescriptive accounting concepts are intended to help accountants analyze unfamiliar situations and develop procedures to account for those situations.

2. ( ) A top-down approach to developing accounting concepts begins by examining the practices currently in use.

3. ( ) In conventional accounting, transactions are recorded in terms of the historical number of dollars received or paid.

4. ( ) In 19X1, $400 was paid to purchase items A and B when the price index was 105. It would take $476 to purchase items A and B in 19X4 if the price index was 125.

5. ( ) Historical cost/constant purchasing power accounting uses a general price index to restate the conventional nominal dollar financial statements.

6. ( ) In current cost accounting, there is no distinction between monetary and nonmonetary assets and liabilities.

7. ( ) When assets and liabilities are reported at their current selling prices, stockholders' equity represents the net liquidation value of the business.

8. ( ) Monetary assets are adjusted for general price-level changes on an historical cost/constant purchasing power financial statement to reflect changes in the price level that occurred since the assets were acquired.

Problem II

You are given several words, phrases, or numbers to choose from in completing each of the following statements or in answering the following questions. In each case select the one that best completes the statement or answers the question and place its letter in the answer space provided.

_____ 1. One of the major components in the FASB's conceptual framework is:

    a. The conservatism principle.
    b. *Statements of Financial Accounting Standards.*
    c. Definitions of important financial statement elements.
    d. The bottom-up approach to developing descriptive concepts.
    e. Selling price valuations.

_____ 2. Current cost accounting:

    a. Is based on the conclusion that current liquidation price is the appropriate valuation basis for financial statements.
    b. Matches with current revenues the current costs to replace the resources consumed to earn the revenues.
    c. For inventories, productive capacity, cost of sales, and depreciation is required of all U.S. companies.
    d. Has become the primary valuation basis for published financial statements of U.S. companies.
    e. None of the above.

_____ 3. A nonmonetary asset was purchased for $25,000 when the general price index was 125. Five years later, when the general price index was 175, the amount that should be shown for the asset on a historical cost/constant purchasing power balance sheet is:

   a. $17,857.
   b. $25,000.
   c. $31,250.
   d. $35,000.
   e. $43,750.

_____ 4. Which of the following is not an example of a nonmonetary item?

   a. Intangible assets.
   b. Land.
   c. Product warranty liabilities.
   d. Notes payable.
   e. Office equipment.

_____ 5. The price index for 19X1 was 112. Prices increased 25% by 19X4. The price index for 19X4 is:

   a. 80.
   b. 100.
   c. 125.
   d. 137.
   e. 140.

_____ 6. In preparing a historical cost/constant purchasing power balance sheet, which of the following categories must be adjusted from nominal dollar amounts to historical cost/constant purchasing power amounts?

   a. Monetary assets.
   b. Nonmonetary assets.
   c. Monetary liabilities.
   d. All assets.
   e. All liabilities and equities.

Problem III

Many of the important ideas and concepts discussed in Appendix D are reflected in the following list of key terms. Test your understanding of these terms by matching the appropriate definitions with the terms. Record the number identifying the most appropriate definition in the blank space next to each term.

_____ Current cost

_____ Historical cost/constant purchasing power accounting

_____ Historical cost/nominal dollar financial statements

_____ Monetary assets

_____ Monetary liabilities

_____ Nonmonetary assets

_____ Nonmonetary liabilities

_____ Purchasing power gains or losses

1. An accounting system that adjusts historical cost/nominal dollar financial statements for changes in the general purchasing power of the dollar.

2. Assets that are not claims to a fixed number of monetary units, the prices of which therefore tend to fluctuate with changes in the general price level.

3. In general, the cost that would be required to acquire (or replace) an asset or service at the present time. On the income statement, the numbers of dollars that would be required, at the time the expense is incurred, to acquire the resources consumed. On the balance sheet, the amounts that would have to be paid to replace the assets or satisfy the liabilities as of the balance sheet date.

4. Conventional financial statements that disclose revenues, expenses, assets, liabilities, and owners' equity in terms of the historical monetary units exchanged at the time the transactions occurred.

5. Fixed amounts that are owed; the number of dollars to be paid does not change regardless of changes in the general price level.

6. Obligations that are not fixed in terms of the number of monetary units needed to satisfy them, and that therefore tend to fluctuate in amount with changes in the general price level.

7. The gains or losses that result from holding monetary assets and/or owing monetary liabilities during a period in which the general price level changes.

8. Money or claims to receive a fixed amount of money; the number of dollars to be received does not change regardless of changes in the purchasing power of the dollar.

Problem IV

Complete the following by filling in the blanks.

1. As business practices have evolved over the years, generally accepted accounting principles (developed prior to the FASB's conceptual framework project) have become less useful as guidelines for new and different types of transactions because they describe _____ _____ ; they do not necessarily describe _____ .

2. If concepts are intended to prescribe improvements in accounting practices, they probably will be developed using the _____ approach, which starts with _____ .

3. Historical cost/nominal dollar accounting is sometimes criticized as being an inadequate response to the problem of changing prices because it does not present _____ in financial statements.

4. Reporting assets at _____ is based on the idea that the alternative to owning an asset is to sell it.

5. Although monetary items are not adjusted on the balance sheet, they can result in _____ _____ during periods of inflation or deflation.

6. _____ represent money or claims to receive a fixed amount of money with the number of dollars to be received remaining unchanged regardless of changes in the purchasing power of the dollar.

7. If the general price index was 115 in 19X1 and was 138 in 19X5, it would be appropriate to say that the _____ had fallen by _____ % from 19X1 to 19X5.

8. The basic reason why conventional financial statements fail to adequately account for inflation is _____ _____ _____ _____ .

9. _____ is the method of accounting that makes adjustments for specific price changes in nonmonetary assets and liabilities.

Problem V

A product that originally cost $20,000 was later sold for $30,000. At the time of sale, the cost to replace the product was $25,500. Also, the general price index rose from 92 at the time of purchase to 115 at the time of sale. Determine the gross profit from sales assuming (1) historical cost/nominal dollar financial statements; (2) historical cost/constant purchasing power accounting; and (3) current cost accounting.

	Historical Cost/ Nominal Dollar Statements	Historical Cost/ Constant Purchasing Power	Current Replacement Cost
Sales			
Cost of sales			
Gross profit			

Problem VI

A company's Cash account showed the following activity and balances during the year:

Balance, January 1	$ 52,000
Receipts from sales	475,000
Payments of expenses	(400,000)
Payment of dividend, December 28	(50,000)
Balance, December 31	$ 77,000

Cash receipts from sales and disbursements for expenses occurred uniformly throughout the year. The general price index during the year was:

January	120
Average during the year	125
December	138

Calculate the purchasing power gain or loss from holding cash during the year.

	Historical Cost/ Nominal Dollar Amounts	Restatement Factor from Price Index	Restated to December 31	Gain or Loss
Balance, January I	$ 52,000			
Receipts from sales	475,000			
Payments of expenses	(400,000)			
Payment of dividend	(50,000)			
Ending balance, adjusted				
Ending balance, actual	$ 77,000			
Purchasing power gain (loss)				

Solutions for Appendix D

Problem I

1. T
2. F
3. T
4. T
5. T
6. F
7. T
8. F

Problem II

1. C
2. B
3. D
4. D
5. E
6. B

Problem III

Current cost 3
Historical cost/constant purchasing
  power accounting 1
Historical cost/nominal dollar
  financial statements 4

Monetary assets 8
Monetary liabilities 5
Nonmonetary assets 2
Nonmonetary liabilities 6
Purchasing power gains or losses 7

Problem IV

1. what accountants currently do, what accountants should do

2. top-down, the objectives of accounting

3. current values

4. current selling prices

5. purchasing power gains or losses

6. Monetary assets

7. purchasing power of the dollar, 16.7

8. that transactions are recorded in terms of the historical number of dollars paid, and these amounts are not usually adjusted even though subsequent changes in prices may dramatically change the value of the items purchased

9. Current replacement cost

Problem V

	Historical Cost/ Nominal Dollar Statements	Historical Cost/ Constant Purchasing Power	Current Replacement Cost
Sales	$30,000	$30,000	$30,000
Cost of sales	20,000	25,000*	25,500
Gross profit	$10,000	$ 5,000	$ 4,500

*$20,000 × (115/92)

Problem VI

	Historical Cost/ Nominal Dollar Amounts	Restatement Factor from Price Index	Restated to December 31	Gain or Loss
Balance, January 1	$ 52,000	138/120	$ 59,800	
Receipts from sales	475,000	138/125	524,400	
Payments of expenses	(400,000)	138/125	(441,600)	
Payment of dividend	(50,000)	138/138	(50,000)	
Ending balance, adjusted			$ 92,600	
Ending balance, actual	$ 77,000		(77,000)	
Purchasing power gain (loss)				$15,600

E Present and Future Values: An Expansion

Learning Objective 1:

Explain what is meant by the present value of a single amount and the present value of an annuity, and be able to use tables to solve present value problems.

Summary

The present value of a single amount to be received at a future date is the amount that could be invested now at the specified interest rate to yield that future value. The present value of an annuity is the amount that could be invested now at the specified interest rate to yield that series of equal periodic payments. Present value tables and business calculators simplify calculating present values.

Learning Objective 2:

Explain what is meant by the future value of a single amount and the future value of an annuity, and be able to use tables to solve future value problems.

Summary

The future value of a single amount invested at a specified rate of interest is the amount that would accumulate at a future date. The future value of an annuity to be invested at the specified rate of interest is the amount that would accumulate at the date of the final equal periodic payment. Future value tables and business calculators simplify calculating future values.

Topical Outline

I. Present value of a single amount

    A. The present value is the amount that could be invested at a specific interest rate to generate a given amount at a definite future date.

    B. A table of present values for a single amount shows the present values of $1 for a variety of interest rates and a variety of time periods that will pass before the $1 is received.

II. Future value of a single amount

    A. The future value is the amount that would be generated at a definite future date if a given present value were invested at a specific interest rate for a given number of periods.

    B. A table of future values of a single amount shows the future values of $1 invested now at a variety of interest rates for a variety of time periods.

III. Present value of an annuity

    A. An annuity is a series of equal payments that are to be received or paid on a regular periodic basis.

    B. Present value of an annuity is the amount that could be invested at a specific interest rate to generate a fund that would be exhausted by a series of payments of a given amount for a given number of periods.

    C. A table of present values for an annuity shows the present values of annuities where the amount of each payment is $1 for different numbers of periods and a variety of interest rates.

IV. Future value of an annuity

    A. Future value of an annuity is the amount that would be accumulated at a given future date if a given series of payments were invested periodically at a given interest rate.

    B. A table of future values for an annuity shows the future values of annuities where the amount of each payment is $1 for different numbers of periods and a variety of interest rates.

Problem I

The following statements are either true or false. Place a (T) in the parentheses before each true statement and an (F) before each false statement.

1. ( ) In discounting, the number of periods must be expressed in terms of 6-month periods if interest is compounded semiannually.

2. ( ) One way to calculate the present value of an annuity is to find the present value of each payment and add them together.

3. ( ) A table for the future values of 1 can be used to solve all problems that can be solved using a table for the present values of 1.

4. ( ) Erlich Enterprises should be willing to pay $100,000 for an investment that will return $20,000 annually for 8 years if the company requires a 12% return. (Use the tables to get your answer.)

Problem II

You are given several words, phrases, or numbers to choose from in completing each of the following statements or in answering the following questions. In each case select the one that best completes the statement or answers the question and place its letter in the answer space provided. Use the tables in your text as necessary to answer the questions.

_____ 1. Ralph Norton has $300 deducted from his monthly paycheck and deposited in a retirement fund that earns an annual interest rate of 12%. If Norton follows this plan for 1 year, how much will be accumulated in the account on the date of the last deposit? (Round to the nearest whole dollar.)

   a. $3,600.
   b. $4,032.
   c. $3,805.
   d. $7,240.
   e. $4,056.

_____ 2. Maxine Hansen is setting up a fund for a future business. She makes an initial investment of $15,000 and plans to make semiannual contributions of $2,500 to the fund. The fund is expected to earn an annual interest rate of 8%, compounded semiannually. How much will be in the fund after five years?

   a. $52,218.
   b. $36,706.
   c. $68,600.
   d. $45,332.
   e. $51,373.

_____ 3. Tricorp Company is considering an investment that is expected to return $320,000 after four years. If Tricorp demands a 15% return, what is the most that it will be willing to pay for this investment?

   a. $320,000.
   b. $177,696.
   c. $182,976.
   d. $ 45,216.
   e. $278,272.

_____ 4. Tom Snap can invest $6.05 for 17 years, after which he will be paid $10. What annual rate of interest will he earn?

        a. 15%.
        b. 9%.
        c. 7%.
        d. 5%.
        e. 3%.

Problem III

Sarah Blue has the three options of receiving $1,000 per year for the next ten years, receiving $6,000 in cash immediately, or receiving $10,000 in cash after five years. Assuming that the current interest rate is 10%, and that Blue wants the option that yields the highest present value, which option should she choose?

Problem IV

Complete the following by filling in the blanks. Use the tables in Appendix E to find the answers.

1. Leila Turner expects to invest $0.83 at a 7% annual rate of interest and receive $2 at the end of the investment. Turner must wait _____ years before she receives payment.

2. Jim Ables expects to invest $5 for 35 years and receive $102.07 at the end of that time. He will earn interest at a rate of _____ % on this investment.

3. Jan Meyer expects an immediate investment of $1,067.48 to return $100 annually for 25 years, with the first payment to be received in one year. This investment will earn interest at a rate of _____ % per year.

Fundamental Accounting Principles, Fourteenth Edition

Solutions for Appendix E

Problem I

1. T
2. T
3. T
4. F

Problem II

1. C
2. A
3. C
4. E

Problem III

The present value of $1,000 received annually for ten years discounted at 10% equals $6,145. The present value of $6,000 received now is $6,000. The present value of $10,000 to be received five years from now is $6,209. Therefore, Blue should choose to receive $10,000 five years from now.

Problem IV

1. Table E-1 shows that when the interest rate = 7% and the present value of 1 = 0.4150 ($0.83/$2), the number of periods = 13.

2. Table E-2 shows that when the number of periods = 35 and the future value of 1 = 20.4140 ($102.07/$5), the interest rate = 9%.

3. Table E-3 shows that when the number of periods = 25 and the present value of 1 = 10.6748 ($1,067.48/$100), the interest rate = 8%.